LIMITS TO THE WELFARE STATE

LIMITS TO THE WELFARE STATE

An inquiry into the realizability of socioeconomic and
political desiderata in a highly industrialized society.

G. J. VAN DRIEL
J. A. HARTOG
C. VAN RAVENZWAAIJ

Martinus Nijhoff Publishing
Boston / The Hague / London

Distributors for North America:
Martinus Nijhoff Publishing
Kluwer Boston, Inc.
160 Old Derby Street
Hingham, Massachusetts 02043

Distributors outside North America:
Kluwer Academic Publishers Group
Distribution Centre
P.O. Box 322
3300 AH Dordrecht, The Netherlands

Library of Congress Cataloging in Publication Data

Driel, G   J   van.
    Limits to the welfare state.

    Bibliography: p
    Includes index.
    1. European Economic Community countries –
Economic conditions – Mathematical models.
2. European Economic Community countries – Economic
policy – Mathematical models. 3. Environmental
policy – European Economic Community countries –
Mathematical models. 4. Welfare state – Mathematical
models. 5. Interindustry economics. I. Hartog,
J.A., joint author. II. Ravenzwaaij, C. van,
joint author. III. Title.
HC241.2.D67   330.9'4'055   79–18060
ISBN 0–89838–026–X

Printed in the United States of America.

PREFACE

In the wake of the publication of Forrester's *World Dynamics* and Meadow's *The Limits to Growth*—books which in The Netherlands may have received excessive attention from the public at large—the Netherlands Organization for Applied Scientific Research (TNO) established a commission under the chairmanship of the late Professor R. Timman. The commission received the task of trying to find a sound philosophical basis for world modelling and to stimulate the building of models that incorporated those aspects of society which are usually left out of mathematical models because of technical difficulties. The study that is discussed in this text was started under the auspices of the TNO commission. Timman died early in 1975. The commission then came under the chairmanship of Professor P. de Wolff. TNO generously provided the means to acquire the computer time necessary to continue our study.

We also wish to express our gratitude to the Statistical Office of the European Communities (SOEC) for their willingness to put the necessary data at our disposal in a form suitable for computer processing. Mr. H. Krijnse Locker's expert knowledge in the field of input-output statistics has especially been of great support to us.

We are much indebted to Professor A.P.J. Abrahamse for his interest in our work and for all the valuable comments and corrections we received from him.

v

We are grateful to Mr. P. van Batenburg, Mr. F. Bisschoff van Heemskerk and Mr. C. Bongers for programming and computational assistance. Finally, we should like to express our great appreciation for the careful and dedicated typing of the manuscript by Mrs. Marga Vermaat.

The authors
Rotterdam
January 1979

CONTENTS

LIMITS TO THE WELFARE STATE

INTRODUCTION

This text contains a study of the industrial heart of Western Europe, the *Region* lying within a radius of 300 kilometers around Rotterdam, consisting of The Netherlands, Belgium, Nordrhein-Westfalen and France Nord. In this Region nearly 45 million people are living and working within an area of 115,000 square kilometers. It is a densely populated, homogeneous, highly industrialized area, which, when viewed from its perimeter must resemble a jumble of smoke stacks and pollution to the environmentalist and look like the promised land to the business executive and the labour leader. We believe it to be similar to the other few concentrations of modern heavy industry in the United States and Japan.

The impact of the conflicting demands on the resources of this economy— providing for economic growth, pollution abatement, increasing the standard of living, economizing on the use of energy and raw materials—was to be studied by means of a model, which had to be versatile enough to incorporate different points of view concerning crucial aspects of the economy. We have constructed a sectoral economic dynamic model in which the capital sector, as is customary, drives the economy forward. Labour is assumed not to be a scarce factor; capital is the only one.

The nucleus of the model consists of the set of balance equations that have become well known under the name of *input-output relations*. We have chosen

1

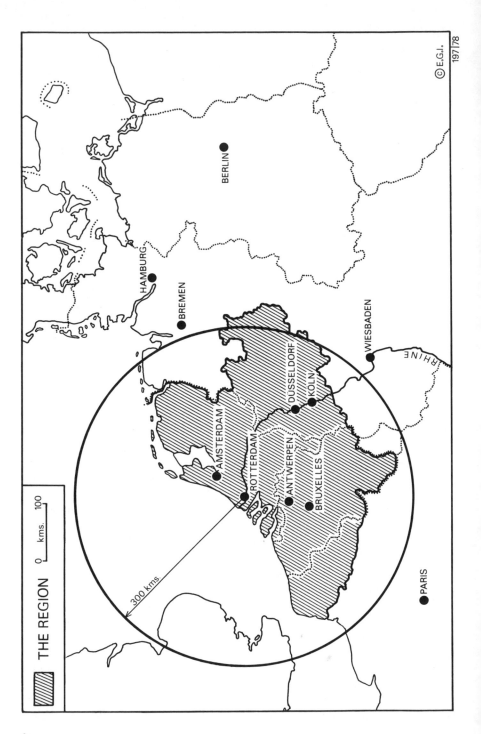

THE REGION

0   kms.   100

300 kms

BERLIN

HAMBURG

BREMEN

WIESBADEN

RHINE

AMSTERDAM

DÜSSELDORF

KÖLN

ROTTERDAM

ANTWERPEN

BRUXELLES

PARIS

© E.G.I.
197/78

2

to build an input-output model because we believe this technique has both relevance and rigour. We thus had to start constructing a technology matrix for the
Region. The Statistical Office of the European Communities (SOEC) published
the harmonized national input-output tables for Germany, France, The Netherlands and Belgium for the year 1965, classified into 56 branches. For our purposes, such a classification was too detailed. We had to aggregate the branches
into a smaller number of sectors in such a way that those branches possessing the
same input structure were classified into one group. For, if dissimilar activities
are aggregated into the same sector, one cannot hope to obtain technical coefficients that are reasonably stable in time. Unfortunately, all necessary data for
the two provinces Nordrhcin Westfalen and France Nord, were published by
SOEC in a classification already aggregated into 17 sectors. This forced us
to adopt the SOEC classification. But we were able to show by means of a
factor analysis that the SOEC classification did not differ too much from the
optimal one.

The Region can only be considered as one homogeneous unit, if the technology matrices for the various (parts of) countries are not essentially dissimilar.
We used analysis of variance techniques to investigate this aspect, the general idea
being to compare the differences in the technical coefficients of the activities
aggregated within each sector with the differences in the technical coefficients of
that sector in several countries. Our findings were that the data do not indicate
that the four national technology matrices under study are essentially different,
and it was therefore meaningful to construct one and the same technology
matrix for the whole Region.

If an emission model is adopted for pollution, it becomes possible to link the
economic aspects of pollution and its control to the technology matrix. To this
end, five rows were added to the matrix of technical coefficients—one for each
kind of pollution we distinguished. The elements of such a row indicate the size
of the abatement costs per dollar output of each of the sectors for the relevant
kind of pollution. This implies that the *value* of the various kinds of pollution is
measured by means of their abatement costs. Furthermore, five columns were
added to the new technology matrix, with one column for each kind of pollution. The elements of each column measure the inputs of conventional commodities needed to abate one dollar of pollution.

The set of dynamic balance equations was completed by matrices of capital
and depreciation coefficients. Data on these coefficients not being available, we
had to construct them ourselves. The vintage model approach was used for this
purpose. We adopted the assumption that these coefficients would be constant
in time, which in a growing economy implies technical progress.

We decided not to follow the approach known as *dynamic Leontief type models.*

We realise that this implies the loss of a beautiful theoretical tool, but the hypotheses underlying this theory are too restrictive for our purpose. In our approach the set of balance equations was made part of a linear programming problem, where an objective function has to be optimized in order to determine the time paths of sectoral production, consumption and investments. This allowed for the possibility of making the model more realistic by introducing additional restrictions of a socioeconomic nature representing political desiderata. Of course, new restrictions will tend to narrow the solution space such that we cannot continue ad infinitum in this respect. But the choice of these restrictions is almost unlimited. As an example, we have chosen a few restrictions subject to much discussion nowadays, but which can easily be replaced or supplemented by others—even in different variables. This possibility makes our model a flexible tool, adaptable to many purposes, such that the model might be viewed as the beginning of a relations-bank.

We have not tried to construct and incorporate behavourial relations, equations that describe the actions of economic subjects. Instead, we have formulated policy desiderata in the form of inequalities. For instance, we introduced the constraint that the capital stock in each sector is not to be decreased in time. Other examples are the inequalities describing the pollution control objectives. In fact, the amount of *nuisance* (i.e. unabated pollution) is decreased at a rate of 10 percent per annum, the amount of nuisance thus being halved in about 7 years.

To complete the model, an objective function had to be specified. Every objective function corresponds with a specific set of time paths of the variables, which is optimal with respect to that function. The choice of such a function is highly subjective. We have chosen to maximize the *total wage sum*, because employment is of paramount importance in political discussions nowadays. Another choice that comes to mind immediately is *total income*. Nowadays we have algorithms that enable us to use multicriteria objective functions, which would have enriched the model considerably. However, we did not incorporate this refinement.

It should be emphasized that we did not try to describe how the economy of the Region was actually operating, nor did we attempt to predict and discuss its future development. If specific values were proposed for a given year's investments in a sector, we did not describe how this result was achieved. Where rules were formulated about pollution control, there was no indication of how the government would enforce these rules; we only investigated whether the system would be capable of complying with these rules in a technical sense, in the sense that the demands of the system not exceed the production capacity.

In this study, our *period of interest* is about 7 years. This time horizon is also used in some recent Dutch government publications in related fields. However, the optimization period of the objective function does not have to be equal to the period of interest.

It is perhaps realistic to plan successively for 1-year periods, assuming a year is necessary to implement investment decisions. In that case, the system lacks a future and sees no need to provide for one, and no goods are available for investment purposes. Thus, we had to add equations to the model, which represented investment decisions. This was done in a separate investment model that was linked to the production model, from which it received information about the relative scarcity of capacity in the sectors (by means of shadow prices) and about the availability of investment goods. The investment model allocates the available resources for expansion of the capacity of the sectors. If the shadow prices are the only compass by which investment decisions are guided, the performance of the model is very poor indeed. These prices are evidently too short-sighted (reflecting only the situation existing at a given moment) to be of much value as a regulatory device. As an experiment, we introduced the size of the sectoral production capacities as an extra regulator, which improved the performance of the system considerably. We only experimented with this variant of our model by using a very condensed version consisting of three conventional sectors and one abatement sector only. Because of the system's poor performance, it was considered to be unnecessary to repeat the computations with the full model.

In the other version of the model, optimization was performed over a 10-year period, the 10-year total of the wage sums being the objective function. Then the model has a structure that is nearly block-diagonal, with about 1000 restrictions. Again, capital investment provided the dynamics of the system. The greater the annual investments, the larger the growth of industrial capacity and the greater the optimal value of the objective function. The size of investments is limited by technical restrictions such as available initial capacity, as well as political desiderata such as more consumption and pollution control. There is no need for a separate investment model. The system itself is able to take the investment decisions, for now it has a future to provide for. Taking the period of optimization to be some years longer than the period of interest, ensures reasonable behaviour of the system in the final years of this period of interest.

It is to be understood that the optimum computed in this fashion is only a theoretical one that can never be attained in the real world. The time paths of the variables are very sophisticated; for instance, investment takes place in sectors where excess capacity already exists. Such investments can be advantageous only in the context of plans covering a longer period. Practical management no doubt generally operates on a lower plane of efficiency, because it is faced with uncertainty.

Part I of this text contains the theoretical details of our study as described in the preceding paragraphs, while Part II deals with the actual computations and results. Part II begins with an account of the statistical research performed to specify and estimate the balance equations. After that, we experiment with the model by introducing various combinations of political desiderata. For each scenario, we examine the feasibility of the model and the behaviour of the system. Starting from the situation in which the only political restrictions are the diminuation of nuisance at a rate of 10 percent annually, together with the maintenance of the level of consumption, we add successively—in a sequence of simulations—new relations to the model restricting the system more and more.

One result seems to be that in a modern, highly industrialized society with its concomitant claims on production capacity on behalf of a growing final demand and on behalf of improving the environment, the annual growth rate of the wage sum can (theoretically) reach some 6 percent if investment policy is planned and executed perfectly.

With the introduction of a limitation of the growth of the production of energy to 2 percent annually, the picture becomes somewhat gloomier. At this point, a theoretical maximum employment growth rate of only 3 percent is suggested.

I THEORY

1 A LEONTIEF TECHNOLOGY FOR THE REGION

1.1. THE CHOICE OF AN INPUT-OUTPUT TECHNOLOGY

As stated in the introduction, we decided to construct a sectoral model having a nucleus consisting of the well-known Leontief balance equations. These equations describe how each commodity's total production in the Region is distributed over the categories of destination (i.e., the intermediate deliveries to other production units, final consumption, gross capital formation and export). We were led to this choice by the conviction that the input-output approach is one of the few disciplines in economics that possess both relevance and rigour — relevance in the sense of the applicability of the theoretical concept, thus having a well-established counterpart in the real world, and rigour in the sense of logical consistency of the theory.

The main sources of input-output data are the United Nations (UN) publications and those of the Statistical Office of the European Communities (SOEC). Both organizations construct harmonized input-output tables for a range of countries. The UN publications are the most widely used, but nevertheless we opted for the SOEC tables. In fact, we had no choice. Since we had to construct a technology matrix for an area not only consisting of nations but also of parts of Germany and France, we needed national data as well as regional data referring to those subregions in a classification corresponding to the input-output tables for the nations. Only the SOEC could serve us in this respect. However, we are not unhappy with the enforced choice. On the contrary, the SOEC tables have some properties that served us well. The most important one is that on behalf of the construction of their tables, the SOEC has put a great effort into defining homogeneous units of production. Here it is not appropriate to go deeply into the details of input-output accounting techniques, but taking "the enterprise" — in the sense of a legally defined organisation with a private balance sheet and subject to a directing authority—as a basic unit for the input-output tabulation, would have presented serious disadvantages. This is because the vertical and horizontal integrations, which often arise in a haphazard manner, result within these units in combinations of activities that vary widely in time within the same country and in space among the countries. Enterprises must first be unravelled into a set of basic units of production. SOEC started from the basic unit of "economic activity", which by definition:

> relates to enterprises or parts of enterprises – even if separated in space – which contribute to the exercise of one and the same activity, characterized by the nature of goods and services produced or by the manufacturing process, this activity being defined in a nomenclature of activities.[1]

Using the concept of homogeneous activities, the general criterion for classification is to regroup activities relating to production of goods and services in branches, on the basis of similarity of the production costs. Constructing input-output tables according to this principle causes many statistical problems, but the advantages are worth the effort. The user of such input-output tables may expect that the technical coefficients derived from them will be relatively stable in space as well as in time.

Although we do presume the reader to be familiar with the usual input-output model, we shall present it here to introduce the notation used throughout this work and to explain a technical adjustment of the model. We shall start with a diagrammatic representation of the input-output table. Centrally placed is the matrix X of intermediate deliveries, whose columns describe the production processes or technologies that convert inputs into output. This matrix is square because of the one-to-one correspondence between activities (columns) and commodities (rows), obtained by the SOEC by means of a proper classification of the activities as well as of the commodities. On the right-hand side of the matrix X one finds column vectors representing the categories of final destination for each commodity, whereas underneath the matrix X one finds row vectors of primary inputs for each activity. In the upper part of the diagram, flows of output from the production units, or its counterpart flows of money towards these units can be read horizontally. The vector of actual production of the goods equals the

| Matrix X of Intermediate Deliveries | Vector f of Final Consumption | Vector g of Gross Investments | Vector e of Exports | Vector x of Actual Production |

Vector m' of Imports

Vector z' of Value Added

Vector x' of Actual Production

sum of the elements of the rows in the matrix X (in matrix notation Xi, if i is a vector with all elements equal to 1) and the vectors of final consumption, gross capital formation and exports. In the left-hand part of the diagram the vertical elements represent flows of money, the payments by the enterprises and its counterpart, the flows of inputs on behalf of the production process. Here, the vector of actual production equals the sum of intermediate inputs ($i'X$) and the vectors of imports and value added. In more detailed input-output tables the so-called transfers might have been added as an additional row vector in the table to reach the equality of row and column totals. We do not want to go into this statistical accounting detail. Furthermore, some of the row and column vectors in the diagram will be disaggregated onto matrices. For our purpose, this process is only of importance for the vector of imports and for the vector of gross capital formation.

Imports might be specified according to delivering foreign branches in the same way as domestic intermediate deliveries. Now, it is a well-known fact that large countries such as Germany and France have lower import ratios than smaller countries such as The Netherlands and Belgium. This does not imply, for instance, that the Dutch and the German technologies differ. According to our definition, technologies only differ if they have different input ratios for a given commodity. Whether this commodity is imported or domestically produced is irrelevant. For the receiving branch it is of little consequence whether they use domestic or foreign goods and services for production. Furthermore, when aggregating countries into a larger region, significant amounts of imports will become domestic goods. Dividing countries into parts, the opposite might be true as well.

Technologies described by intermediate deliveries inclusive of imports are not influenced by this type of aggregation or by import substitution. They therefore lend themselves better to international comparison and the construction of the technology matrix for a multination region. The SOEC tables have the advantage of giving the complete specification of the imports. Actually, they are presented in the same table as the domestic intermediate deliveries, but in separate rows. However, the inclusion of imports in the matrix **X** on behalf of the stability of the technology has consequences for the system. The diagrammatic representation of the input-output table now becomes:

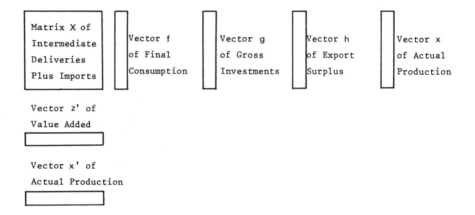

In the vertical flow of payments nothing has been changed from the preceding diagram. To ensure that the row totals equal the column totals, one has to subtract the vector of imports from the vector of exports, thus leaving as a last term in the rowwise addition the export surplus. The horizontal balance equation of the system, using the notation of the diagram, is:

$$x = Xi + f + g + h$$

One can assume that in every branch the values of the inputs relative to the value of actual production in that branch are constants. These constants are called *technical coefficients* and are denoted by a_{ij}:

$$a_{ij} = \frac{x_{ij}}{x_j} \quad \text{or} \quad Xi = Ax$$

Substituting **Ax** for **Xi**, one obtains the Leontief balance equations in its familiar form:

$$x = Ax + f + g + h$$

The matrix **A**, as well as all vectors appearing in this equation, can be derived directly from the input-output tables; thus, they are all known quantities. As soon as the Leontief equations are used in a dynamic model, the vectors need a time index. In that case, it is useful to rewrite the vector of gross capital formation. Following Leontief we shall split up this vector in two components, in the following way:

$$g_t = Dx_t + K(x_{t+1} - x_t)$$

The elements of the matrices **D** and **K** will be called *depreciation coefficients* and *capital coefficients*, respectively, in conformity with the term *technical coefficients* as a name for the elements of the matrix **A**. We shall return in detail to the significance for the model of the matrices **D** and **K** in Section 1.5.

As a final remark on the construction of the matrix of technical coefficients, we mention that the SOEC presents their tables with a valuation in so-called prices ex-works/ex-customs. We do think that this kind of valuation is the best for our purpose, but we do not intend to discuss the valuation problem in input-output accounting.

Now it is one thing to have at one's disposal sets of input-output tables of separate countries, but it is another thing to aggregate them into one table for the whole Region and to apply the result in the framework of a dynamic Leontief system. We first have to face this set of problems, as will be done in the next two sections.

1.2 ON THE AGGREGATION OF THE SOEC INPUT-OUTPUT TABLES

Introduction

The 1965-input-output tables published by the SOEC were given in a classification of 56 branches for five of the member countries: Germany, France, Italy, The Netherlands and Belgium. Unfortunately, these tables were only available for the countries as a whole, while we were interested in those for Nordrhein-Westfalen and France Nord, the two "provinces" that together with The Netherlands and Belgium were defined to constitute the Region. For these two provinces data on employment were available, published, however, by the SOEC in a condensed classification of 17 sectors. The aggregation key for the 56 branches into the 17 sectors is provided by the SOEC. It raises no difficulties, except for a few details. By means of the employment data it was possible to construct regional input-output tables using linear interpolation.

The principles governing the condensation of input-output tables with elements measured in value units, are explicitly formulated by Dorfman, Samuelson and Solow[2] as: "we should try to classify industries so that those that we aggregate together are industries requiring the same types and relative quantities of input for their production" or "that production of all the constituent parts of the aggregate invariably changes in about the same proportion". The first requirement – that we should aggregate industries that have a similar input structure – is the criterion we have adopted in this section. This criterion is supported by Malinvaud[3] too. He states: "the above analysis shows that similarity of technical conditions may provide us with a sufficient reason for aggregation, even when the commodities produced are somewhat different".

The criteria that are used by the statisticians who are responsible for constructing aggregated input-output tables are not always clear. The SOEC, for instance, simply states:[4]

> the Working group 'Economic aggregates and statistical indicators at regional level', . . . has defined the nomenclature of the branches to be followed for working out in detail the economic aggregates at the regional level. This nomenclature in 17 branches . . . is used in the present publication to present several industrial statistics.

That is all. Why the material is condensed into 17 aggregates (we shall call them *sectors* to distinguish them from *branches,* although the difference is only gradual) and why the sectors are defined the way they are, remains completely obscure. But the names that were given by the SOEC to these sectors suggest that it was not always the similarity of the input structure that determined the aggregation process. Though we were obliged to accept the aggregation as it was performed by the SOEC, it is of vital interest to know to what extent their classification in 17 sectors satisfies our aggregation criterion. Therefore, we decided to investigate how far and in what way we could condense the 56 branches of the NACE code using the requirement that we form aggregates out of those branches that do have a similar input structure.

If we make the criterion "a similar input structure" operational by translating it into "a highly correlated input structure", the technique of factor analysis becomes the obvious tool to perform the aggregation. Factor analysis is meant to bring forth the common parts in sets of data, in our case in the columns of a technology matrix. It is remarkable that in a recent article by Kymn,[5] five selection methods on behalf of an optimal aggregation key are discussed, all of which in our opinion possess a more indirect character than the straightforward method to be presented here.

A Factor Analytic Model for Aggregation

It will be necessary to start by defining some scalars and matrices. The symbol m will be used for the number of branches in the NACE code, that is, the number of rows and columns in the technology matrices that have to be studied. Following a notation by Malinvaud, the symbol M will be used to represent the number of common factors, that is, the number of aggregates that can be distinguished following the chosen method. Let A be a technology matrix of order m by m and Z the same matrix standardized. This standardization is performed by computing means and standard deviations for each column of A. Subtracting from each element of A its column mean and dividing the result by $\sqrt{m}$ times the column standard deviation, gives the corresponding element of Z. Because of this standardization, it does not make any difference whether the computations are based on an input-output matrix or on a technology matrix. The advantage of the standardization is that the matrix R of correlations between pairs of columns, can simply be written as $R = Z'Z$.

Now, according to the method of factor analysis we shall split up the matrix Z as follows:

$$Z = FL + U$$

We shall interpret the columns of the (m by M) matrix F as *basic technologies*, that is, as the technologies of the aggregates. The (m by m) matrix U denotes the *matrix of residuals*. The elements of the (M by m) matrix L are weights. Therefore, each element of Z—thus each technical coefficient—is to be viewed as a weighted average of technical coefficients of the basic technologies, with a random term added. In statistical parlance, the matrix F is usually called the *matrix of factor scores* and the matrix L the *matrix of factor loadings*. If the magnitude of the residuals in the matrix U (measured by their sum of squares) is small compared to the sum of squares of the elements of Z, we can say that the factor analysis has been successful. The large number of columns of Z can be replaced by a small number of columns of F.

It will be obvious that by this representation the matrices F and L are not unambiguously defined. If one defines $F^* = FT^{-1}$ and $L^* = TL$ as the matrices of factor scores and of factor loadings, respectively, the matrix of residuals is left unaffected:

$$U = Z - FL \quad \text{as well as} \quad U = Z - F^*L^*$$

This is an essential aspect of the factor analytic model, but (unique) determination of F and L will become possible with additional restrictions. One restriction can be made without any loss of generality: diag $(F'F)$ = diag (I). This implies that the "length" of a common factor will be equal to 1, just like that of each of the standardized columns of Z. Thus, basic technologies are standardized in the same way as the original ones.

In general, there are no reasons to restrict oneself to orthogonal factors, but here there are. The rationale of aggregation lies in the correlations between technologies. By inverting this rationale we state that no further aggregation is meaningful as soon as only uncorrelated technologies remain.

We shall make further use of the indetermination of a factor analytic solution to try to fulfill two aims. For a meaningful interpretation of the factor analytic model it is desirable that all substantial factor loadings have a positive sign. As the factors represent basic technologies, negative loadings of observed technologies upon these factors are difficult to interpret. But it is also desirable that each of the variables has only one (very) high factor loading, because only this will enable us to classify the variables obviously according to their corresponding basic technology. The *varimax rotation*—a method widely accepted in factor analytic applications—tends to satisfy both aims. It transforms a given matrix of factor loadings to a new one, such that the sum of the variances of the squares of the factor loadings for each row of the matrix is a maximum. The mathematics involved to find this rotation are of no importance for a better understanding. We may refer to the standard literature.[6]

One of the most widely used techniques in factor analysis is the method of *principal components*. The rationale of this method is often given by geometrical arguments. Because of the peculiar character of the data (the distribution of the elements within a column of an input-output matrix is always very skew), these geometrical arguments are not applicable in our situation. We therefore prefer to introduce the method as a special case of component analysis, the latter resulting from a general objective. One may formulate this objective to find an initial solution of F and L, with diag $(F'F)$ = diag (I), as:

$$\text{Minimize tr } (Z - FL)'(Z - FL)$$

This way of derivation of the method of principal components by means of a minimization rather than a maximization procedure, was already given by Whittle,[7] with but one difference—namely, F defined as a vector instead of a matrix. If F is a matrix the derivation is a little more cumbersome, but the advantage is that the indetermination of the solution is included as an integral part of the method.

As will be demonstrated in Section 4.1, our method of deriving a classification of branches into sectors works quite well. There are striking similarities as well as divergences between the SOEC classification and the factor analytical one, which lead us to conclude that aggregation could have been done better for our purposes than it actually is. Taking this into account we proceed to the next stage.

1.3 INTERNATIONAL AND INTERTEMPORAL COMPARISON OF TECHNOLOGY MATRICES

Introduction

In this section we describe the method by which we have investigated possible similarities among the technology matrices of the countries involved: Germany, France, The Netherlands and Belgium such that we may be able to speak of one technology for the Region. Thereafter, some remarks will be made concerning the intertemporal comparison of technology matrices. A procedure will be formulated to test for stability over time in these matrices.

In contrast with the methods we have found in the literature, our method is a statistical one — it is couched in terms of a stochastic character. It must be emphasized that statistical arguments, always falling within the realm of induction, are never capable of furnishing proofs the way mathematics does in the world of deduction. The strongest conclusion to be drawn by statistical reasoning is that, on the basis of the hypothesis under test, the observed values of the variables being studied are improbable. It is then customary to *reject* the hypothesis. If the observations are not improbable, then the hypothesis is *accepted.* A series of 20 throws with a coin, all resulting in heads, does not constitute proof of bias of the coin. But it does make this bias very probable. In our case, we will show that the data do not contradict the hypothesis of equality of the technology matrices, which leads us to accept this equality as a basis for further work. But we have not proven this equality in the traditional sense. It might have been that the matrices are really different, but that by mere chance the observations are more in accordance with the hypothesis of equality. Stochastic arguments are not very powerful, but they can function in a world that might be inaccessible without them.

International Comparison by Analyzing Variances

Given an aggregation key of the 56 branches of the NACE-CLIO code into 17 or any other number of sectors, the input-output tables on the basis of these sectors can be constructed for each country involved, and the construction of aggregated matrices of technical coefficients is then only a matter of simple calculations. Once these matrices have been constructed, we have to answer the question of whether they are sufficiently similar to enable us to use one and the same technology matrix for the Region. One way to answer this question is to compare the variation among the countries of each of the technical coefficients with some standard. We emphasize that the use of some standard is inevitable because there will nearly always exist some differences in comparable technical coefficients among countries, thus leading to the trivial conclusion that technologies are not exactly the same.

Several methods have been developed to construct a criterion that can be used to determine whether two or more technology matrices have to be considered to be essentially similar.[8] We have attempted to construct a statistical test based on a well-known statistical method designed to analyse differences in population means. This technique is called *analysis of variance,* commonly abbreviated as ANOVA, and is one of the most widely used and successful tools of statistical analysis. It is described in many excellent textbooks.[9] We shall only describe the method to the extent necessary for an understanding of our argument. In this section we will use the so-called *one-factor model* in which each observation is assumed to consist of the true value of a constant with a random error superimposed.

For our purposes, we prefer not to start the exposition of the one-factor ANOVA model with the four aggregated technology matrices of order 17 by 17 that we actually intend to compare, but rather we will begin with the four original technology matrices of order 56 by 56. Let the symbol a_{ijk} $(i, j = 1, \ldots, 56;$ $k = 1, \ldots, 4)$ indicate the observation contained in the cell at the intersection of the ith row and the jth column of that technology matrix of country k. First we aggregate the rows of each of the country matrices so that we obtain four rectangular 17 by 56 matrices with typical element a_{Ijk} $(I = 1, \ldots, 17; j = 1, \ldots, 56;$ $k = 1, \ldots, 4)$. Aggregation of the rows is performed by adding together those rows that belong to the same sector:

$$a_{Ijk} = \sum_{i \subset I} a_{ijk}$$

It does not matter whether the coefficients a_{ijk} differ for various delivering branches $i \subset I$, but as a consequence of the similarity of the technical coefficients of the branches aggregated into the same sector, the coefficients a_{Ijk} for various receiving branches $j \subset J$ $(J = 1, \ldots, 17)$, ought to be the same except for random errors. It is thus assumed that each of the elements a_{Ijk}, given I and k, can be written as:

$$a_{Ijk} = \bar{a}_{IJk} + \epsilon_{Ijk}.$$

Therefore, each a_{Ijk} consists of the true coefficient $\bar{a}_{IJk}$ and a part ϵ_{Ijk} due to a random error. Note that these a_{Ijk}'s, the elements of a rectangular matrix of order 17 by 56, are the *observations* on which the analysis is performed.

The standard assumption underlying ANOVA is that ϵ_{Ijk} is a random drawing[10] from a normal distribution with zero expectation and variance σ_{IJ}^2 for all $j \subset J$ and for all four k. The null hypothesis states that the four quantities $\bar{a}_{IJk}$ are all equal to $\bar{a}_{IJ}$. On behalf of the statistical test, two more concepts have to be introduced. The first one will be denoted by $\hat{a}_{IJk}$, defined as:

$$\hat{a}_{IJk} = \frac{1}{n_J} \sum_{j \subset J} a_{Ijk}$$

where n_J is the number of branches in aggregate J. This coefficient represents for country k the mean value of the technical coefficients classified under a given combination of I and J.

The second concept will be denoted by $\hat{a}_{IJ}$ and is defined as the unweighted mean of the country means $\hat{a}_{IJk}$:

$$\hat{a}_{IJ} = \frac{1}{4} \sum_k \hat{a}_{IJk}$$

Each $\hat{a}_{IJk}$ is to be viewed as an estimate of the (national) $\bar{a}_{IJk}$. The same can, of course, be asserted for the observed technical coefficient a_{IJk}, computed via straightforward aggregation of the (56 by 56) input-output matrices. The difference is that the latter is a weighted instead of an unweighted average of the a_{Ijk}'s ($j \subset J$). If these a_{Ijk}'s are similar, the difference between weighted and unweighted averages will be of no practical importance.

In order to test the null hypothesis that all $\bar{a}_{IJk}$'s are equal to $\bar{a}_{IJ}$, the test statistic F_{IJ} is calculated as follows:

$$F_{IJ} = \frac{_aS_{IJ}^2}{_wS_{IJ}^2}$$

with:

$$_aS_{IJ}^2 = n_J \sum_k \frac{(\hat{a}_{IJk} - \hat{a}_{IJ})^2}{3}$$

and with:

$$_wS_{IJ}^2 = \frac{1}{4} \sum_k \sum_{j \subset J} \frac{(a_{Ijk} - \hat{a}_{IJk})^2}{(n_J - 1)}$$

The quantity $_aS_{IJ}^2$ is usually called the *variance among countries* and the quantity $_wS_{IJ}^2$ the *variance within countries*. Both variances are estimates of σ_{IJ}^2. The variance among countries is brought on common base with the variance within countries by multiplying the variance of the four means $\hat{a}_{IJk}$ by n_J, the number of branches aggregated into the sector J.

One must realise that σ_{IJ}^2 as it is defined here, can be viewed as the sum of two independent terms: namely, a component due to measurement errors and a component due to inevitable aggregation inaccuracies. These inaccuracies are inevitable because no two activities are exactly the same. Any aggregation of the 56 branches into a smaller number of sectors produces this kind of variation. The detailed analysis in Section 4.2 shows that the latter variance is far from negligible in many sectors, but this has to be accepted as soon as one constructs a national condensed technology matrix. It is therefore our opinion that the variance among countries has to be compared with the sum of both components of variance, that is, with the total variance within countries and not with the variance due to the errors of measurement only. The question we are trying to answer is whether the aggregation over the countries introduces a significant additional source of variance, due to a country effect.

If the null hypothesis is true, the probability distribution of the F-statistic (F-ratio) is known. Tables of this distribution are readily obtainable. With the help of such a table one can find the probability, assuming the null hypothesis is true, of observing an F_{IJ} at least as large as the computed value. If that probability is small, it is customary to reject the null hypothesis. It will be obvious that in principle we have to compute an F-ratio for every combination of I and J in which $n_J \geqslant 2$. In fact, we should have to compute some 200 F-ratios. This implies that we have to take into account the fact that even if the null hypothesis were true, some F-ratios might be significant by mere chance. Actually, we expect that if the null hypothesis is true, about 5 percent of all F-ratios will be significantly high at the 5-percent level; similar statements hold for the 10-percent and the 25-percent levels. This also means that a few very high F- ratios do not really contradict the null hypothesis.[11]

We therefore had to adapt the common statistical practice.[12] An obvious procedure would be to construct a frequency diagram of the observed F-ratios and to test whether the observed frequencies correspond with the theoretical ones. Since the distribution of an F-statistic depends on its pair of degrees of freedom and one of these parameters, namely $4(n_J - 1)$, will have different values for different J, this procedure is impracticable. However, using the tables of the F-distribution, one can classify each observed F-ratio as being significant or not, at a chosen level. In this fashion we can count the number of F-ratios that are significant at the 5-percent level, between the 5- and 10-percent levels, between the 10- and 25-percent levels and below the 25-percent level, respectively. Under the null hypothesis, the observed frequencies of these F-ratios (one for each combination of I and J with $n_J \geqslant 2$), can be seen as a sample from the multinomial distribution with parameters .05; .05; .15 and .75.

The agreement between the observed and the expected frequencies of the F-ratios can be ascertained by means of a goodness-of-fit test. The sum of the standardized squared differences between the observed and the expected frequencies is approximately distributed as a chi-square (χ^2) statistic with 3 degrees of freedom. If the agreement is poor, the probability that the χ^2-statistic exceeds the observed χ_o^2, is small. If we decide that this probability is too small, we shall have to reject the null hypothesis that the $\bar{a}_{IJk}$ are equal to $\bar{a}_{IJ}$ for all k and we shall conclude that the variance among countries is (significantly) higher than the variance within countries. If not, the best (statistical) estimate for the technical coefficients in the Region is the unweighted mean of the corresponding coefficients in the constituent parts.

We emphasize that the test procedure had to be done in two steps: the determination of the right-tail probability of each of the F-ratios and the subsequent classification of these probabilities in some chosen categories, followed by the testing of the obtained frequency distribution over the categories. This results in a one-dimensional rejection region for the null hypothesis.

In Section 1.2, an optimal aggregation scheme by means of factor analysis has been introduced. The aggregation into 17 sectors as it was executed by the SOEC, therefore, is suboptimal from this point of view. In the optimal aggregation scheme, the variance within the countries is minimal on the average, this being an alternative formulation of the objective underlying the aggregation procedure. Comparatively small differences among countries might manifest themselves more easily as being significant by using the factor analytical aggregation scheme rather than using the SOEC one. On the other hand, by using the SOEC aggregation scheme, differences among countries might be exaggerated just because of the suboptimality of the aggregation procedure. Therefore, it is difficult to predict which classification scheme is the best point of departure for investigating differences among countries. We decided to analyse both of them.

As will be shown in the empirical part of this book in Section 4.2, the conclusions are unmistakable: there is no statistical reason to believe in real differences in technology among the four countries under investigation. Therefore, considering each national technology matrix as an estimate of the technology for the Region, we computed the unweighted average of these four technology matrices.

Some Notes on Intertemporal Comparison

Every 5 years the SOEC publishes detailed input-output tables that become available with a time lag of 5 years. This means that we had at our disposal the 1965 and the 1970 tables. Unfortunately, however, the SOEC changed the classification in which the 1970 tables were published in such a fashion that it proved to be impossible to convert it simply into the 1965 classification. This necessitated the making of a further condensed classification. Herein is the reason why we investigated separately the differences, if any, among the input-output tables of different countries in the given year 1965 and the possible differences between the input-output tables in the different years 1965 and 1970. Without the complication caused by the change in the classification schemes, it would have been much more satisfactory to investigate the two effects simultaneously, that is, the country effect and the time effect in the parlance of the statisticians. Because of the inevitable inaccuracies and all other problems to which the conversion of the classification gave rise, we thought it advisable to perform the country comparison separately.

We do not think it is useful to present here the formulae of more complicated ANOVA schemes. The interested reader can find them in the standard literature. We should like to confine ourselves to the remark that we assumed all interactions to be zero, because the amount of data often was restricted and because there are few a-priori reasons to assume significant interactions. Under this assumption it is possible to separate the sum of squares in components and to test for each of three effects: country effect, time effect and branch effect.

As far as the difficulties mentioned allow us to draw any conclusions at all, these conclusions are that there is scarcely a country effect and not the slightest indication of a time effect. In less technical terms, the data do not indicate that the matrices of the four countries differ significantly and they certainly do not suggest that the matrices change over time. In all these results we find the justification for assuming one technology matrix, not only for the different countries but also during the 10 years that will become the time span of our investigation.

1.4 POLLUTION AND ITS ABATEMENT

Production and consumption react on the environment by withdrawing from it energy and raw materials and by deteriorating the environment. The first aspect will be treated in a later chapter, where we will study some consequences of limiting the rate of growth of the consumption of energy. The latter aspect, pollution and its abatement, will be the subject of this section.

It is of course no new concept that enterprises strive to limit the negative effects on the environment of their activities. In some cases they have done so voluntarily, in other cases they were forced to do so by provisions of the law. Therefore, the input-output tables have always contained costs pertaining to these efforts, but in general it is impossible to isolate them. On the other hand, much pollution is left unabated. There exist many reasons why enterprises have been unwilling to undertake the arduous task of eliminating all adverse influences upon the environment of their activities. The required technology might have been unavailable or the competitive position might have been too vulnerable, while much knowledge of the harmful secondary effects of some economic activities is still fragmentary and certainly of recent date.

We included the amount of unabated pollution as one of the variables in our model. From our point of view this "nuisance" is an imposed and undesired "final demand", a commodity with a negative utility. If nuisance consists of noise and smell, it has to be "consumed" in the area. Poisonous substances may be "accumulated" in the area. Air and water pollutants may be "exported" across the border. In other words, the final destination of nuisance consists of the same categories as does the final destination of conventional commodities. The product of the pollution abatement activities, which of course has a positive utility, will be called *clean environment.*

It will be obvious from the preceding remarks that we decided to treat the pollution problem by means of the *emission* approach instead of by the *immission* approach. The reason behind this choice is twofold. In the first place, the emission approach is the much simpler one. But more important is the fact that because of the choice of our Region—a fairly homogeneous, densely industrialized area—the problem of the spatial distribution of the nuisance is relatively unimportant, as are the effects of pollution imported from outside the Region. The pollution of the river Rhine by waste from the potassium mines in France is an exception to this last point.

In an emission model the nuisance can be evaluated at its abatement costs. It is not necessary to determine who the damaged party is, nor to what extent this is the case. The great advantage of such a model is that nuisance only depends on the size of the production of abatement sectors. We have taken our pollution data from a study of the Dutch Central Planning Bureau. We have to confess that much more time and effort was spent examining the conventional data provided by the SOEC than was spent on evaluating the pollution data, mainly because this subject lies outside of our field of expertise. We shall return to this matter in Section 4.3.

To handle the discharge of some well-defined residuals connected with the production of conventional goods, rows and columns are added to the matrix of technical coefficients. As we distinguished five different pollutants, also five rows and columns were added. The elements of each extra row are the abatement costs per unit of the production value of the conventional sectors for a certain pollutant generated in the different production processes of the activities.

The columns that are added to the matrix of technical coefficients create *dummy sectors* representing the five activities *abatement of pollution.* The elements in the upper part of each column are the technical coefficients that represent the relative expenses on conventional goods needed to abate one unit of the pollution concerned. The abatement sectors pollute also. It is well known, for instance, that an activity such as water pollution control creates solid waste as an unwanted residual; thus, the abatement sectors themselves give rise to abatement costs too. These are incorporated in the lower part of the columns in exactly the same way as is done for the conventional sectors. The addition of rows to a technology matrix suggests that there are "new" sectors in the economy, delivering a commodity that is required for the production of conventional goods. Viewed from another angle we may interpret such a row as a special kind of primary input, comparable with indirect taxation. Actually, the pollution rows occupy an in-between position. Insofar as pollution abatement does take place, the first interpretation is entirely correct. The delivered good is clean environment, a commodity not more abstract than some of the services already incorporated in modern technology. However, if pollution abatement is neglected, the latter interpretation holds.

A new matrix of technical coefficients is the result of this approach. It again is a square matrix and can be partitioned as follows:

$$\begin{bmatrix} A_{11} & A_{12} \\ A_{21} & A_{22} \end{bmatrix}$$

where:

A_{11} contains the technical coefficients of the conventional sectors
A_{12} contains the technical coefficients of the abatement sectors
A_{21} describes the pollution by conventional sectors, valued at its abatement costs
A_{22} describes the pollution by abatement sectors, valued at its abatement costs.

Referring to the symbols introduced in Section 1.1, denoting nuisance by the symbol f_a and using the subscript c for conventional variables and the subscript a for abatement variables, the Leontief relations transform to:

$$x_c = A_{11}x_c + A_{12}x_a + f_c + g_c + h_c$$

and

$$x_a + f_a = A_{21}x_c + A_{22}x_a$$

The meaning of the last equality is that the sum of the abated pollution x_a and the nuisance f_a (the unabated pollution) equals total generated pollution. If nuisance is transferred to the right side to achieve a more usual notation, it appears with a minus sign. As can be verified, the vectors x_c and x_a can be solved for and expressed in terms of the vectors of final demand. This solution equals the necessary size of the production of conventional and abatement sectors, given a predetermined level of the final demand of conventional goods and an admissible level of nuisance.

The model does not indicate in which way these targets will be achieved, nor how the predetermined levels of final demand will be enforced. Therefore, it is not relevant at this point to speculate about the way in which the pollution abatement should be financed. The fact that abatement costs appear in the technology matrix might be interpreted to imply that enterprises have to finance these costs. This is not true; whether the costs will be paid from the profits of the enterprises or will be financed by some authority by means of a system of subsidies, remains undecided in our model.

1.5 ESTIMATION OF CAPITAL COEFFICIENTS

Introduction

In the Leontief equation in Section 1.1, gross investments g_t have been split up into depreciation and net investments:

$$g_t = Dx_t + K(x_{t+1} - x_t)$$

In this section we are concerned with the determination of the elements of the matrices D and K. The available input-output tables that permit us to calculate the technical coefficients a_{ij}, do not contain the necessary information to do the same for the depreciation coefficients d_{ij} and the capital coefficients k_{ij}. For this purpose one should need the complete input-output tables in two successive years with gross investments subdivided into depreciation and net investments and moreover, both vectors completely specified according to their destination, the receiving sectors. For this reason, the estimation of K and D has to be performed by a rather cumbersome detour.

To this end, we refer in the first place to the well-known concept of *capital-output ratios*. Let the value of the capital stock of investment good i, held by sector j at the beginning of year t available for the production in that sector, be denoted by c_{ijt}. The (partial) capital-output ratio $\bar{k}_{ijt}$ (a bar is put above k to distinguish temporarily these ratios from the corresponding coefficients in the Leontief equation) is then defined as:

$$\bar{k}_{ijt} = \frac{c_{ijt}}{x_{jt}} \qquad (1.5.1)$$

Because the capital stock is expressed in value units, aggregation over the several kinds of investment goods is possible and the capital-output ratio for sector j is to be defined as:

$$\bar{k}_{jt} = \sum_i \frac{c_{ijt}}{x_{jt}}$$

Finally, the sector ratios may be averaged (x_{jt} being the weights) to obtain the capital-output ratio for the total economy; a concept often used in theoretical work.

To facilitate the comparison of the capital-output ratios $\bar{k}$ and the capital coefficients k, we shall start making the assumption that all partial capital-output ratios are constant in time, at least for a certain time span, so they will not carry a time index. The possible development of the ratios in time is influenced by two well-defined effects, namely, the technological change that tends to lower the ratio and the deepening of capital (the rising amount of capital per worker) that tends to raise it. Historical evidence shows that in the past century the overall capital-output ratio was remarkably stable, at least in the long run. To quote Samuelson[13]: "either by coincidence, or as the result of some economic mechanism that needs study, technological change has just about offset diminishing returns to capital accumulation". This observation was based on a study of "great trends of economic development for America in this century" and concerned the total economy. It is not certain that it also holds for separate sectors. Since the overall ratio is a weighted average of the sector ratios, relative output per sector being the weights, it could be possible that in all sectors technological change dominated the effect of capital deepening such that all sector ratios will decrease, but that at the same time, changes in the economical structure of production will occur in favour of sectors with a relatively high capital-output ratio, leaving the overall ratio unchanged. The converse might be the case as well. But even so, the sector ratios would only change slowly, for the effects of technological change and capital deepening are opposite and, moreover, these changes take their time. As we only work with a 10-year horizon, we feel entitled to assume constant capital-output ratios.

Now, returning to the Leontief equation and assuming that gross investments are specified as to destination, we may write:

$$g_{ijt} = d_{ij} x_{jt} + k_{ij}(x_{j(t+1)} - x_{jt})$$

The partial capital stock $c_{ij(t+1)}$ by definition equals last year's stock c_{ijt} plus gross investments minus depreciation during the past year:

$$c_{ij(t+1)} = c_{ijt} + (g_{ijt} - d_{ij} x_{jt}) \times 1$$

As c has the character of a stock and g and x are flows per year, the constant of

1 year is necessary to get the dimensions correct. From this formula it follows by recursion:

$$c_{ij(t+1)} = \sum_{\tau=0}^{\infty} (g_{ij(t-\tau)} - d_{ij}\,x_{j(t-\tau)}) \times 1$$

Obviously, this sum converges. Eliminating $g_{ij(t-\tau)}$ gives:

$$c_{ij(t+1)} = \left\{ k_{ij} \sum_{\tau=0}^{\infty} (x_{j(t+1-\tau)} - x_{j(t-\tau)}) \right\} \times 1 = 1 \times k_{ij}\,x_{j(t+1)}$$

Because the constant 1 is expressed in years, the dimension of the capital coefficient k_{ij} is 0. Numerically, k_{ij} is equal to the capital-output ratio $\bar{k}_{ij}$, which becomes obvious if the present formula is compared with Formula (1.5.1); but k_{ij} is a pure number and $\bar{k}_{ij}$ is expressed in *years*.

That the capital coefficients have to be pure numbers can also be seen if one changes the period in which production (and thus investments) are measured, from 1 year to 1/2 year, letting the period in which the investment decisions are converted into capital stock remain 1 year (2 periods). Then the only significant difference in the Leontief specification would be the change in the time span. This is true because production as well as investments are approximately halved. Therefore, an element k_{ij} of **K** must describe something like the ratio of "annual services offered by the capital stock" to annual production. It is not really the capital stock but its continuing annual services on behalf of production, that we are describing by k_{ij}. On the other hand, capital-output ratios do have the dimension *time*. This will be evident because the same change of the time period has no effect on the value of the capital stock but it halves the value of production, which implies a doubling of the capital-output ratio. Supposing that the unit of time is 1/2 year and applying the same algebra as before, one finds:

$$g_{ijt'} = d_{ij}x_{jt'} + k_{ij}(x_{j(t'+2)} - x_{jt'})$$

and

$$c_{ij(t'+1)} = k_{ij}(x_{j(t'+2)} + x_{j(t'+1)}) \approx 2k_{ij}x_{j(t'+1)}$$

then

$$k_{ij} \approx \frac{1}{2}\bar{k}_{ij}$$

It is only because the time span in which investment decisions are converted into capital stock equals 1 year, that we can exchange capital coefficients by capital-output ratios and that the numerical values of k_{ij} that we need can be estimated as $\bar{k}_{ij}$. Henceforth, the bar over the symbol k will be omitted.

Estimating capital output ratios for sectors implies estimating the value of the capital stock owned by the enterprises that belong to that sector. For a national economy, the classification of the capital stock according to sectors and to kinds of investment goods is a very interesting datum in itself. If these statistics were available—for instance, as a result of a census among all enterprises—the capital-output ratios could be derived directly. Unfortunately, these kinds of data are scarce and the coherent set we need is not at our disposal. We therefore had to construct these ratios in an indirect way, making use of a separate model and of time series that were suitable as well as available. This model is a so-called vintage model.

A Vintage Model for the Capital Stock

The basic assumption underlying the vintage model is that the capital stock for the investment good i in every sector j, consists of goods that have constant (economic) lifetimes of θ_i years. At the beginning of the year t, the value of the available stock c_{ijt}, therefore, equals the sum of gross investments (in price terms of the year t) in the year $t - \theta_i$ up and to including $t - 1$.

$$c_{ijt} = g_{ij(t-1)} + g_{ij(t-2)} + \ldots + g_{ij(t-\theta_i)}$$

The assumption of constant capital-output ratios permits the substitution of $k_{ij}x_{jt}$ for the left-hand side of this expression:

$$k_{ij}\, x_{jt} = \sum_{\tau=1}^{\theta_i} g_{ij(t-\tau)} \tag{1.5.2}$$

In general, more or less detailed data on investments are only known for the year for which the input-output tables are constructed. Time series of real investments per investment good and per sector (in the relevant classification) are not available. However, the trend in the development of total investments per sector is useful to approximate the sum in the right-hand side of Formula (1.5.2). If gross investments show a perfect regular trend with annual growth rate α_j, so that:

$$g_{ijt} = (1 + \alpha_j)\, g_{ij(t-1)} \tag{1.5.3}$$

then the capital stock is equal to:

$$c_{ijt} = \sum_{\tau=1}^{\theta_i} g_{ij(t-\tau)} = \sum_{\tau=1}^{\theta_i} \left(\frac{1}{1+\alpha_j}\right)^{\tau} g_{ijt} \tag{1.5.4}$$

In reality, annual investments in a sector behave rather irregularly and its trend is hidden behind large errors of estimate. Still the right-hand side of Formula (1.5.4) may serve to approximate the capital stock. The estimation of the α_j's is based on the time paths of real production of the sectors instead of those of investments in them. With constant capital-output ratios, the growth rates of real production and real investments are the same.

Elaboration of Formula (1.5.4) yields the estimation formula for the partial capital coefficients:

$$k_{ij} = \frac{g_{ijt}}{x_{jt}} \frac{(1 + \alpha_j)^{\theta i} - 1}{(1 + \alpha_j)^{\theta i} \alpha_j} \tag{1.5.5}$$

With the assumptions underlying this result, the depreciation coefficients can be found too. In the vintage model, depreciation in year t equals the recent value of the investment goods put out of use; thus,

$$g_{ij(t-\theta_i)} = \frac{1}{(1 + \alpha_j)^{\theta i}} g_{ijt}$$

Related to the value of present production, the partial depreciation coefficients are defined and estimated as:

$$d_{ij} = \frac{g_{ijt}}{x_{jt}} \frac{1}{(1 + \alpha_j)^{\theta i}} \tag{1.5.6}$$

As can be verified, the magnitudes of k_{ij} and d_{ij} for $\alpha_j \to 0$ tend to the trivial values:

$$k_{ij} = \frac{g_{ijt}}{x_{jt}} \theta_i \quad \text{and} \quad d_{ij} = \frac{g_{ijt}}{x_{jt}}$$

For all α_j, an easy check on computations consists of:

$$\alpha_j k_{ij} + d_{ij} = \frac{g_{ijt}}{x_{jt}}$$

The expression on the right-hand side of this equation is the sectoral partial investment quota. In Figure 1.1, a *nomogram* is presented in which one can read at once the ratios of k and d with respect to this quota mentioned. These ratios are denoted by k^* and d^*, respectively; the subscripts i and j have been omitted. As will be shown in Section 4.4, the sectoral partial investment quota will be split up into two components on behalf of the calculation of the capital and depreciation coefficients:

$$\frac{g_{ijt}}{x_{jt}} = \frac{g_{ijt}}{g_{jt}} \times \frac{g_{jt}}{x_{jt}} = \omega_{ij} \lambda_j \quad \text{with} \quad g_{jt} = \sum_i g_{ijt}$$

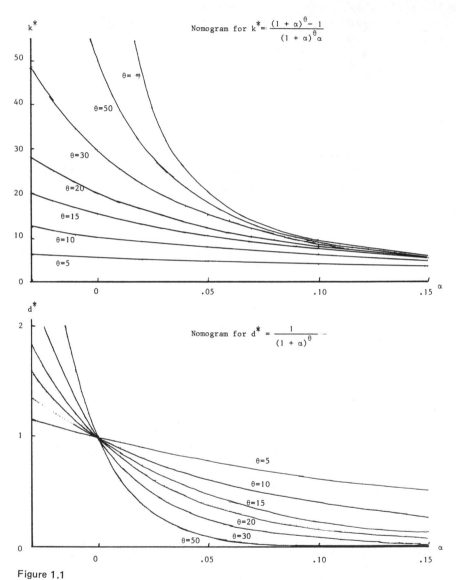

Figure 1.1

where λ_j is the sectoral investment quota and ω_{ij} is an element of the investment-dispersion matrix; both coefficients are assumed to be independent of t. The estimation formulae for k_{ij} and d_{ij} therefore will be:

$$k_{ij} = \omega_{ij} \lambda_j \frac{(1 + \alpha_j)^{\theta_i} - 1}{(1 + \alpha_j)^{\theta_i} \alpha_j} \tag{1.5.7}$$

$$d_{ij} = \omega_{ij} \lambda_j \frac{1}{(1 + \alpha_j)^{\theta_i}} \tag{1.5.8}$$

The parameters λ_j and ω_{ij} are directly derived from statistical tables from the SOEC and some supplementary information within the framework of their 1965 input-output investigation. Apart from knowledge about these parameters, the construction of the matrices $\mathbf{K}$ and $\mathbf{D}$ requires two types of estimates. The first ones are the lifetimes θ_i of each kind of investment good. Although in practice we shall sometimes distinguish θ_i for the receiving sectors as well, thus leading to a notation θ_{ij}, we did not want to bother the reader with so much detail in this exposition. The second type of estimates are the rates of growth of real production per sector. The θ_i's have to be guessed and the α_j's will be estimated from a period just before the year 1965, but the choice of the number of years considered is rather arbitrary. For this reason, we shall finish our treatment of the construction of capital coefficients in the next paragraph with a short discussion of the effects of a wrong guess of the θ_i's and α_j's.

Effects of Errors in Lifetimes and Rates of Growth

According to Formulae (1.5.5) and (1.5.6), k and d are proportional to the investment quota. Errors in this quantity enter relatively to the same extent into the calculated coefficients. The effect of a mistaken rate of growth on k and d can be examined by means of the partial elasticities of k and d, with respect to α. These elasticities are defined as:

$$\epsilon(k,\alpha) = \alpha \frac{\partial(\ln k)}{\partial \alpha} \quad \text{and} \quad \epsilon(d,\alpha) = \alpha \frac{\partial(\ln d)}{\partial \alpha}$$

Both elasticities are negative. Overestimation of the rate of growth of real production in a sector implies underestimation of k and d. However, as $|\epsilon(k,\alpha)|$ proves to be smaller than 1, the effect of an erroneous rate of growth on k is kept within bounds. As can be seen in Table 1.5.1, where the elasticities with respect to α are summarized for some values of α and θ within their relevant ranges of magnitude, the effect on d of errors in α is stronger, especially for the combination of a large value of both α and θ.

Table 1.5.1. Partial Elasticities of k and d with Respect to θ.

	$e(k,\alpha)$ θ (in years)					$e(d,\alpha)$ θ (in years)				
	5	10	15	30	50	5	10	15	30	50
$\alpha = -0.02$	-0.06	-0.12	-0.17	-0.35	-0.60	-0.10	-0.20	-0.31	-0.61	-1.02
$\alpha = -0.02$	-0.06	-0.10	-0.15	-0.28	-0.42	-0.10	-0.20	-0.29	-0.59	-0.98
$\alpha = 0.05$	-0.14	-0.24	-0.34	-0.57	-0.77	-0.24	-0.48	-0.71	-1.43	-2.38
$\alpha = 0.10$	-0.26	-0.43	-0.57	-0.83	-0.96	-0.45	-0.91	-1.36	-2.73	-4.55

Table 1.5.2. Partial Elasticities of k and d with Respect to θ.

	$e(k,\theta)$ θ (in years)					$e(d,\theta)$ θ (in years)				
	5	10	15	30	50	5	10	15	30	50
$\alpha = -0.02$	1.05	1.10	1.16	1.33	1.59	0.10	0.20	0.30	0.61	1.01
$\alpha = 0.02$	0.95	0.90	0.86	0.73	0.59	-0.10	-0.20	-0.30	-0.59	-0.99
$\alpha = 0.05$	0.88	0.78	0.68	0.44	0.23	-0.24	-0.49	-0.73	-1.46	-2.44
$\alpha = 0.10$	0.78	0.60	0.45	0.17	0.04	-0.48	-0.95	-1.43	-2.86	-4.77

The corresponding elasticities with respect to θ can be derived in the same way.

$$\epsilon(k,\theta) = \theta \, \frac{\partial(\ln k)}{\partial \theta} \quad \text{and} \quad \epsilon(d,\theta) = \theta \, \frac{\partial(\ln d)}{\partial \theta}$$

As can be seen in Table 1.5.2, the effect of an error in θ on k is positive and again kept within bounds for expanding sectors. The partial elasticity $\epsilon(d,\theta)$ is nearly the same as $\epsilon(d,\alpha)$, so the same remark as before can be made about the effect of an error in θ on d.

It appears that using the vintage model, with rates of growth in general between 0.02 and 0.10 as we found, the computed capital coefficients are reasonably insensitive for not too severe errors in the parameters of α and θ. The (total) relative error in k, due to the combination of relative errors of 1 percent in both α and θ, is (much) smaller than 1 percent if the errors in α and θ are made in the same direction—that is, if both parameters are either overestimated or underestimated. To see this, one simply has to add the partial elasticities for k with respect to α and θ. In the other case, if both errors are made in the opposite direction, the relative error in k is always about 1 percent.

Regarding the depreciation coefficients, their computed values are more questionable. If for growing sectors the errors in α and θ are made in the opposite direction, the situation is not serious. In the computed value of d, the partial effects will cancel. If on the other hand the errors in α and θ are made in the same direction, the partial effects will cumulate and this might get out of control. In that case the computed depreciation coefficients have a limited significance, albeit only for those investment goods with a long duration of life (such as buildings) in the fast growing sectors.

Note that in our formulation of the model, the depreciation coefficients will be added to the technical coefficients into one matrix $(\mathbf{A} + \mathbf{D})$ (see Section 2.2), so the possible errors in d will be diluted and we dare state that, except perhaps for a single element, the errors in the matrix of depreciation coefficients cannot be too serious.

2 THE MODEL
Presentation and Justification

2.1 THE SCOPE OF THE STUDY

The set of Leontief balance equations presented in the preceding chapter, has been the subject of extensive study. Often the assumption of no-excess capacity is added, so that the vector $\mathbf{x}$ of actual production equals the vector $\mathbf{w}$ of production capacity in every year. Under this assumption the Leontief relations may be rewritten as:

$$\mathbf{w}_t = (\mathbf{A} + \mathbf{D})\,\mathbf{w}_t + \mathbf{K}(\mathbf{w}_{t+1} - \mathbf{w}_t) + \mathbf{v}_t$$

where the vector $\mathbf{v}_t$ is defined as the sum of final consumption $(\mathbf{f}_t)$ and export surplus $(\mathbf{h}_t)$. Rearranging terms we get:

$$\mathbf{K}\mathbf{w}_{t+1} = (\mathbf{I} + \mathbf{K} - \mathbf{A} - \mathbf{D})\,\mathbf{w}_t + \mathbf{v}_t$$

Assuming $\mathbf{K}$ to be nonsingular for reasons of simplicity:

$$\mathbf{w}_{t+1} = \mathbf{K}^{-1}\left\{(\mathbf{I} + \mathbf{K} - \mathbf{A} - \mathbf{D})\,\mathbf{w}_t + \mathbf{v}_t\right\} \tag{2.1.1}$$

The maximum rate of growth inherent in this set of first-order difference equations, given certain initial values $\mathbf{w}_0$ and given a set of vectors $\mathbf{v}_t$, is studied for instance by the Indian economist Chakravarty.[1] It is quite understandable that in a developing country such as India, the attention of the government—planning economic policy—will be mainly focussed on the creation of those circumstances that will permit maximum economic growth. Viewed in this light, it is easy to see that an author such as Chakravarty will concentrate especially on the analysis of total production required, to realise a given vector of final demand in the static case and on investments in the dynamic one. In this light, the (dynamic) input-output model is used as an accounting framework to demonstrate "the equilibrium result of particular planning decisions",[2] where "planning" is meant to be "planning for growth".

In the modern welfare state, however, the word *planning* is not used in so restricted a sense. The attention is not focussed anymore on growth alone, although it must be stressed that in general one seems to underestimate the economic and social problems that arise at the transition to a less expansive economy. One can conquer the inertia, inherent in large organisations such as national education systems and industrial labour and employers' unions, only with great effort and after a considerable delay. Nevertheless, one gradually begins to pay more attention to the "quality of life" of the individual, now and in the future. Raw material and energy problems, pollution and similar problems on the one hand, aid to underdeveloped countries, maintaining the standard of living, nivellation of the income distribution on the other hand, are issues receiving much attention from the public as well as from governments.[3] The model behind Formula (2.1.1), however, does not lend itself naturally to the incorporation of these considerations. But it can be easily modified to do so, albeit at a certain cost.

The requirement of complete utilisation of capacity is introduced because of mathematical considerations. For the consequences resulting from dropping this assumption, we may refer to Chakravarty.[4] The assumption is not a very realistic one, which will become obvious if one realises that the increase of the capacity of an activity requiring inputs from other activities will have to remain unused where these latter activities are already employed to full capacity. The mathematical consequences of a transition to inequalities will be that one transfers from the world of difference equations to that of optimization models. This is because the freedom of movement—the consequence of the dropping of the no-excess capacity assumption—must be fenced in, to make possible the derivation of meaningful assertions from the model. In this fashion it becomes practicable to introduce new relations and also new variables to the model, which symbolize further objectives of the planning authorities.

We constructed this (socioeconomic) part of the model in such a fashion that here also the relations maintain their character of being part of an accounting framework. In the Leontief model, production has to be large enough to provide for intermediate deliveries, final demand and capital investment. To these requirements are now added provisions for pollution abatement, while on the other hand, production may not become so large that consumption of scarce resources (such as energy) surpasses certain limits imposed by the authorities.

Here it is perhaps most appropriate to delve somewhat deeper into the nature of our model. Its objective is certainly not to function as a prediction tool, where by the term *prediction* is meant the making of pertinent statements (predictions) about the future. In other words, we do not intend to state what value a given variable will attain at a certain moment of time. If we compute a time series of industrial capacity, for instance, this does not imply that our opinion is that industrial capacity will follow the computed pattern in reality. The only significance of this pattern is that it is the logical consequence of the set of suppositions, which taken together constitute the model.

If we define forecasting as "the process of organized exploratory thinking about the future",[5] we like to see our work as an exercise in forecasting. It is only a tool to help decide whether a complex of economic desiderata is realizable. This contention does not mean that we express an opinion about whether a given target will or can actually be reached. We do not go that far. What we do investigate is whether the system can support the burden dictated by claims made against it by the authorities; in other words, whether production capacity is sufficient to support a given policy proposal. At the same time, we investigate the possible existence of inconsistencies in such a policy proposal; for instance, requiring a given increase in the standard of living but at the same time restricting energy use might be inconsistent. If production capacity is insufficient or if there are inconsistencies in the plan, we classify the plan as *infeasible;* otherwise, the plan is *feasible.* It is a matter of course that if the material requirements—inherent in a given plan—surpass available capacity, that policy cannot be executed—at least as long as a negative balance of payments is excluded.

On the other hand, if the material means are adequate, this does not imply that the policy can be carried out. Only one of the necessary conditions is satisfied. Perhaps the most important one (if necessary conditions can be divided into important and less important ones), but only one out of many. Stated in a different manner, if investments in a given year are computed as amounting to a certain magnitude, we cannot and do not want to indicate what forces bring about the realization of this amount. We only maintain that the objective function will be optimized if the variables are given certain values.

We now present another example. Regarding pollution abatement, we introduce a certain scenario in which nuisance decreases annually with a given percentage. We bypass the whole set of forces that have to be rallied to reach this outcome. At our level of aggregation, the costs of pollution abatement can be financed out of profits. But this is certainly not true on the level of the individual enterprises; however, we do not consider this aspect. We have done this system-

atically by disregarding the whole complex of political factors that determines
the functioning of an economy; it is this set of factors that makes one doubt
whether a consistent policy will ever be feasible.

We have excluded all behavioural relations, that is, relations that describe the
reaction of individuals or the community on impulses from the outside. The reason is not that the combining of behavioural relations with sectoral ones would
be impossible—it has often been done.[6] We felt, however, that it becomes more
and more difficult to have confidence in the usual economic theories—often
built from a neoclassical basis—as descriptions of behaviour in a swiftly changing
economic order in which their fundamental assumptions become steadily less
realistic. Apart from this, we can advance in defence of our choice that economic
theory often has the character of an equilibrium model, while we work with a
dynamic one; or that economic theory is directed towards the very short run as
are the usual trade-cycle theories, while we work with a time horizon of 10 years.

Growth theories in general do lack a sociopsychological foundation,[7] as does
our model or they have been rendered out of date (Marx). We cannot deny that
as a consequence of this line of conduct, the results of our analysis will be of
limited applicability. They can only be viewed as a maximum estimate of what is
feasible, and the discrepancy between this theoretical maximum and the reality
might be appreciable. But the advantages are considerable. In the first place, many
projects have failed because of a too ambitious design. Cherrington's contention:

> In the first instance, it strikes me that there is considerable over-reaching in
> this field, perhaps wider and bigger claims than the state of the art can in fact
> deliver. For example, there are a good many late contracts, a good many
> overrun contracts and a good many contracts which end up with little more
> than junk

contains a lot of truth.

Furthermore, we foster the belief that the conceptual simplicity of our model
will facilitate contact with the final user. To cite the Sussex group once more[8]:

> The real complexity of the problems under consideration—often compounded
> by the apparent complexity of the analytical methods used—can be an
> obstacle to a real dialogue between the policy maker and the analyst.

It is difficult to imagine anything simpler than the balance equations used, which
only confront requirements with availabilities.

The preceding considerations induced us to give the socioeconomic part of the
model the same mathematical character as the first part. All relations will be
defined as inequalities and will be discussed in Section 2.2. The Leontief restrictions are discussed in Section 1.1. Here we can confine ourselves to a broad

verbal description of the remaining restrictions. The restrictions we introduced vary from inevitable limitations, such as the restriction that actual production is not allowed to exceed available capacity, to requirements such as the decreasing of available capacity in any sector is not allowed (a requirement that is only realistic in the case of reasonably strong aggregation), to avowed political desiderata such as the precept that nuisance has to decrease with at least a given percentage.

Henceforth, we shall indicate these three groups of restrictions by the names *capacity restrictions, disinvestment restrictions* and *political restrictions.* This enumeration shows again that the socioeconomic relations inserted into our model bear a rather arbitrary character. They are a translation of some of the objectives enunciated in the already cited Dutch government paper "Selective Growth". Therefore, these restrictions do have a background in practical politics, but they are only meant as an example and can easily be formulated differently or replaced by other ones.

In contrast with the drafting of the Leontief restrictions, the formulation of the socioeconomic restrictions dealt with in this chapter is not a difficult task. One can simply invent them. The laborious construction of the multitude of constants is not necessary, and they are not based on the many assumptions that are required to specify the Leontief relations. Consequently, they are completely different in essence. The Leontief restrictions are in a certain sense inescapable and so are the capacity restrictions. Every policy has to stay within their boundaries. The socioeconomic restrictions miss this trait. It may be that there also exist socioeconomic restrictions that have (in the short run) this feature of inescapability. What these restrictions are, has never been well clarified to our knowledge. Maybe that psychology has formulated laws that are valid within the individual sphere. However, this subject is beyond our field of vision. But in the socioeconomic context the situation is much less apparent: there, the behaviour of the community is derived by aggregating the behaviour of individuals. Since this aggregation process can only be performed quite imperfectly, the consequence is that macroeconomic relations find only an incomplete basis in individual psychology. We have the feeling that the macrobehavioural relations are as a rule derived from the microbehavioural relations by means of analogy arguments.

In drawing conclusions about these somewhat philosophical arguments, we can formulate the purpose and significance of our work as follows. In the Leontief part of the model, great care is spent in constructing and validating the technological coefficients. These, along with the capacity restrictions, determine a feasible area outside of which no possible program exists. By means of an objective function an optimum point can be selected from this set. If one adds additional restrictions — a subject to which we return in Section 2.5 — the optimum will almost certainly not become more favourable and the program might indeed become infeasible. In other words, if a planning authority formulates a plan in terms of socioeconomic desiderata and if such a plan—when translated into mathematical restrictions and welded to our set of technological restrictions— proves to be infeasible, the plan will certainly be unworkable. Anyway, we feel that the burden of proof of the realizability of the plan lies with the authorities in that case. If the plan proves to be feasible, the model may be used to measure the benefits of the plan in terms of a (multicriteria) objective function.

2.2 FORMULATION OF THE MODEL

The aims of the model have been explained in the preceding section, whereas its structure will be investigated extensively in Section 3.3. In the present section it will therefore suffice to present the model formulae of the various groups of restrictions in the linear programming (LP) problem, as it is defined.

The Leontief Restrictions

With the introduction of abatement sectors and a pollution technology in Section 1.4, a distinction is made between conventional sectors (subscript c) and abatement sectors (subscript a). The Leontief equations for the former—describing how actual production (x_c) is distributed over the categories of destination: intermediate deliveries to conventional sectors $(A_{11} x_c)$ and to abatement sectors $(A_{12} x_a)$, final consumption (f_c), gross investments (g_c) and export surplus (h_c)— has been written as:

$$x_c = A_{11} x_c + A_{12} x_a + f_c + g_c + h_c$$

To make the Leontief part of the model dynamic, it is necessary to add a time index and to rewrite g_c:

$$x_{ct} = A_{11} x_{ct} + A_{12} x_{at} + D_{11} x_{ct} + D_{12} x_{at} + K_{11} (x_{c(t+1)} - x_{ct})$$
$$+ K_{12} (x_{a(t+1)} - x_{at}) + f_{ct} + h_{ct}$$

Now according to the preceding section, the equality sign will be replaced by an inequality sign and a distinction will be made between actual production and maximum capacity of production, to be called *capacity*. For capacities, the symbol w is chosen. Thus, the Leontief restrictions for the conventional sectors are:

$$x_{ct} \geqslant (A_{11} + D_{11}) x_{ct} + (A_{12} + D_{12}) x_{at} + K_{11} (w_{c(t+1)} - w_{ct})$$
$$+ K_{12} (w_{a(t+1)} - w_{at}) + f_{ct} + h_{ct} \qquad (2.2.1a)$$

One might argue that the inequality sign in the Leontief relations is rather non-sensical because actual production will always be distributed in some fashion. We will show that it is advantageous to write the relations in this way, because it enables us to specify a "slack" in a Leontief relation. Afterwards, these slacks will be distributed over the categories of final demand as well.

For the abatement sectors it does not make sense to change the equality sign in the Leontief relations into an inequality sign, because for these sectors the relations merely describe to what extent total pollution is abated. Nuisance will not serve as an investment good nor will it be exported. Therefore regarding the abatement sectors, the Leontief relations remain as they were presented in Section 1.4, with a time index added:

$$x_{at} = A_{21} x_{ct} + A_{22} x_{at} - f_{at} \qquad (2.2.1b)$$

The Capacity Restrictions

The distinction between actual production and capacity logically gives rise to the so-called *capacity restrictions:*

$$x_t \leqslant w_t \qquad (2.2.2)$$

holding for conventional and abatement sectors as well. These restrictions are merely implications of the distinction mentioned; they have nothing to do with socioeconomic desiderata.

The Disinvestment Restrictions

The *disinvestment restrictions* that we have incorporated, are describing a certain socioeconomic claim: in no sector will there occur a decrease in capacity. Thus,

$$w_{t+1} \geqslant w_t \qquad (2.2.3)$$

or using the symbol y_t for the capacity expansion $(w_{t+1} - w_t)$, we obtain $y_t \geqslant 0$. As stated in the preceding section, this claim is not very restrictive in a growing economy and not too unrealistic for aggregates so large that the economy consists of only 17 conventional sectors.

The Political Restrictions

These restrictions are dealing with the f_t, that is, final consumption for the conventional sectors and nuisance for the abatement sectors. For the consumption of conventional goods we started with restrictions of the following kind:

$$f_{c(t+1)} \geqslant f_{ct} \qquad (2.2.4a)$$

describing that consumption is not allowed to decrease in any sector. Once more it might be argued that this claim is not very restrictive in a growing economy and not very unrealistic with such "big" sectors. But the set of restrictions could easily be generalized to:

$$f_{c(t+1)} \geqslant (I + H_c) f_{ct}$$

where H_c is a diagonal matrix of which the elements may differ among sectors.

For the nuisance we introduce the following restrictions:

$$f_{a(t+1)} \leqslant (I - H_a) f_{at} \qquad (2.2.4b)$$

stating that the upper level of admitted (unabated) pollution is continuously decreasing at a given percentage annually, for each kind of nuisance. It is our intention to put all elements of H_a equal to 0.1, this value implying a half-life of 7 years for the amount of unabated pollution.

Summary

It should be realised that in our model each kind of restriction gives rise to 22 (in)equalities because there are 22 sectors. Regarding the Leontief restrictions, we shall replace all h_{ct}'s by their initial values h_{c0}, so that the export surplus is kept a constant. Because in a certain year t the capacity for that year is a datum, the set of 88 restrictions in year t is expressed in 66 variables, namely: 22 actual productions (x_t), 22 capacity expansions (y_t), 17 consumptions (f_{ct}) and 5 nuisances (f_{at}). The result of this counting suggests that in no year will *all* restrictions be binding; it is to be expected that only 66 of the 88 will be.

2.3 THE OBJECTIVE FUNCTION

As already mentioned, we introduced an objective function to be optimized in order to eliminate the degrees of freedom left after supplementing the Leontief inequalities with socioeconomic restrictions. This is necessary to ensure that the variables will follow a well-defined path in time.

It is not unrealistic in these days to attach so much weight to employment optimization as to make it the objective of the whole system. We therefore have chosen optimization of total wages as our objective. Again, it can be maintained that technically it is quite simple to replace this objective by any other one.

Should one desire to replace it by optimization of total income, then it is only necessary to change some coefficients, while the solution that optimized the original objective function will not be very far from the optimal one for the other function. If one assumes the wage rate to be constant, optimization of total wages is identical with optimization of employment. Perhaps it will be superfluous to stress that the assumption of a constant wage rate is not essential at all. If one deems this assumption to be untenable, then it is easy to replace it by the assumption that wages increase with a given percentage and, again, the optimizations of total wages and employment are equivalent.

A serious objection that can be levelled against our objective function is that in actual practice the optimization of several criteria will simultaneously be pursued. Even within trade and industry in a capitalist society, firms have more objectives than the pursuance of maximal profits only; even there it can be safely assumed that firms strive after multiple objectives. The realization of this endeavour can then be described by an ordered finite series of numbers. If it should be the case that these numbers represent variables expressed in different units, then one is confronted with serious difficulties. In the simplest case, this situation can be reduced to that of the single objective function by the choice of suitable weights. However, as Lange[9] puts it: "It is not difficult to quote examples, particularly for a socialist economy in which it is not possible to determine directly the weights of particular objectives". Our contemporary society is not so far removed from the socialist one that the same would not be true for our world.

The theory of multiobjective programming has progressed appreciably in the last few years. On the bases of the theory of, for instance, Nijkamp and Spronk,[10] programs have been built that make it possible to use the IBM Mathematical Programming System Extended 370 (MPSX/370) optimization package to solve this kind of problem. These programs, however, became available too late to be incorporated into this study.

2.4 UNCERTAINTY

We decided to include terms representing uncertainty neither in the Leontief nor in the political restrictions. In the Leontief restrictions, stochastic terms might have been incorporated to introduce errors of measurement in the variables. The political restrictions might be couched in a stochastic form, if one should wish to do so.

The reasons that led us to give the relations a deterministic character are associated with the doubtful assumptions underlying the justification and use of stochastic terms in econometric models. The hypothesis that a given variable —as the disturbance term that is customarily included in econometric relations to "explain" the difference between computed and observed values of variables — obeys a stable probability distribution, from which the realisations have to be considered as random drawings, is perhaps the most heroic one that can be made. That this is really so, becomes immediately clear if one realises what care for instance a casino must bestow on ensuring that the outcomes of the roulette wheels obey the homogeneous distribution. One could wonder what are the forces that in "nature" take care that variables obey stable probability laws and that observations of economic variables are random drawings from these distributions. The central limit theorem is most often used in defence. But there is nothing in the assumptions needed for the derivation of the normal law that ensures constancy in time for the parameters.

It is not very amazing that the normal distribution has been successful in describing the distribution of measurement errors of instruments for astronomical observations. Gauss formulated a set of assumptions, perfectly adapted to this field of application, as a point of departure for the establishment of this law. To the best of our knowledge, however, this has never been done in the field of the social sciences. We venture to presume that it is impossible to realise such an endeavour in the light of the great number of eminent scholars who have occupied themselves with this problem. We therefore have to agree with Oscar Lange[11] that "probabilistic and statistical methods of programming have limited practical applications". The approach based on subjective probabilities is a more promising one. But in our situation, where the decision maker is unknown and a fortiori so are his or her utility and subjective probability assessments, this method is inapplicable.

Abandoning the concept of stable probability distributions for stochastic terms in economic relations, the problem of uncertainty might be tackled by the formulation of various scenarios. The term *scenario,* used in this context, is originated by Herman Kahn.[12] There exist several pithy descriptions of the term. One definition is: "A scenario is a sequence of possible events which determine the inputs that are applied to the computer model in order to assess the likely consequences if such events indeed take place."[13] Another definition is:

> Scenarios are plausible and logically consistent views of the future which do not contain a judgement as regards the degree of realizability. When drafting a scenario, the designer's main interest is focussed on whether it is a possible sequence of events, not whether it is a probable one.[14]

The last definition is a precise description of our model.

The building of scenarios is of course not anything new. The utopias are its oldest manifestation. Scenarios have a highly subjective character, they are a product of the imagination. Nevertheless — or perhaps better, just because of that—the method received a great stimulus from the range of techniques the computer has put at our disposal. The second report of the Club of Rome designates the method used in so many words as "scenario-analysis".

It is not appropriate at this time to go into the pros and cons of the scenario technique. We have decided against its rival in research into the future, a range of techniques falling under the heading of "prognosis". In the year 1937, Tjalling Koopmans, one of the great pioneers of the probabilistic method in the social sciences, defends the use of this method in a characteristically modest fashion by explicitly stating that "it may be better to have some point of support obtained by the use of a set of simplifying assumptions, than none at all."[15] The epigones have not all been that careful, and they often lose sight of the real significance of the assumptions underlying the method.

Anyway at the moment there exists an alternative for the probabilistic method, an alternative greatly superior in many ways, the most important one being that regularity assumptions are avoided.[16]

2.5 THE RELATIONS-BANK CONCEPT

In 1953 Goodwin[17] lamented:

> It is a melancholy reflection that, after about a century and a half of intensive effort by a distinguished line of investigators, it is still doubtful, whether we can state any quantitative, empirical law in economics,

a remark as much to the point now as it was then. Many reasons might be brought forth to explain this predicament. Some of them are closely related to the nature of the object of study and are as such inevitable. One aspect of this problem, however, that can be improved using modern technology has not received the attention it deserves in the literature. An important element in the research technique of the physical sciences is that the experiments upon which a certain result is based are extensively reported. This enables others to replicate the experiment and to test it in all its aspects. Only after this process has been performed in extenso, do the experimental results become an intrinsic part of the scientific complex.

The organised database upon which the economic theories were founded, has remained small for a large period of time. It is of course often true that systematic observation of economic life (i.e., the kind of contact the banker or the politician had with his or her object of study during a long lifetime) has led to profound insight into the functioning of society. But that has been the exception only reserved for the true giants, while it is very often their fate not to be recognized as such by their contemporaries who do not have the means to appreciate the profundity of insight of people so superior to them. For the capable scholar there is no place in such a scheme and in the physical sciences it has been this person who had to separate the chaff from the corn—a process that is not always performed without friction. Its negative aspects have been superbly described by Arthur Koestler in his *The Case of the Midwife Toad*. It has nevertheless proved to be essential for the great organised progress of knowledge in this field.

Since the beginning of the thirties, the amount of data available to the economist has been increasing steadily, as has the scale of the necessary computations. We believe it is a fair question to wonder whether the computations and assumptions incorporated in a project such as Tinbergen's *Business Cycles in the U.S.*, have ever been thoroughly checked. It is true that the sources of the series are very conscientiously enumerated, but the independent testing of the material is a task that is not easily performed. The numerical computations require great competence and dedication, to mention but one aspect. It is quite possible that the lack of progress in the social sciences finds part of its explanation in the omission of repetition of experiments. Deeply probing discussions, which are of real assistance to the researcher, are often only possible with colleagues who know the investigation in all its details.

The development of the computer and its peripheral equipment, however, has changed all this radically. It is indeed still true that insight into the quality of the basic data can only be obtained by means of labourious and dedicated research. But the analysis of the material can be greatly facilitated by means of the software packages presently available to the researcher. It is still necessary that the researcher completely master the theoretical aspects of the techniques used, but he or she is not expected to judge the numerical aspects of the software. That is the task of the computing centre with which the researcher works. Replicating and testing the computations now becomes an actual possibility. It is deplorable that the disorder in the computer world detracts from the full fungibility of computer programs written in different languages or for different makes of computer.

The dominant position of IBM fortunately facilitates the exchange of data and programs. For the future there are at least two trends that tend to improve the situation. In the first place, it is to be expected that the number of computer manufacturers will diminish. On the other hand, the improvement of software that makes feasible the linking of models constructed according to different principles is being set in motion at present. This development is known under the name of "model-bank systems".[18] It merits attention because it will enable the economist to keep a certain distance from his data just as it is presently possible for the user of databank facilities. These possibilities are not fully operative at present, but part of the objectives can be reached by using IBM's MPSX/370 package. In The Netherlands, anyway, the package is in a prevalent position.[19] Its most important properties in this context are:

1. It is used widely.
2. The calling of the routines can be part of a PL/I source program.
3. It contains many possibilities for sensitivity analysis by means of parametric procedures.
4. Once sufficient experience with a problem has been acquired so that a reasonable initial solution is known (totally or partially), optimization costs little central processing unit (CPU) time.
5. It is quite simple to copy a problem and its solution and basis onto tape, so that it can be forwarded by mail and investigated someplace else.

This set of properties facilitates experimentation with the model. Changing the model to investigate the consequences is technically simple and relatively inexpensive.

When experimenting with the model, however, a few general rules must be remembered. Suppose the model consists of M restrictions in N variables. M_1 of these restrictions are equalities, M_2 are inequalities. Mathematically the role of the equalities is completely different from that of the inequalities. The equalities decrease the dimensionality of the solution space of the variables. The inequalities do not; they only decrease the content of this space. Suppose further that the objective function is formulated in terms of L variables. In many cases, $L < M_2$. If the optimal solution is unique, it can be formulated in terms of M_2 variables. We have not been able to formulate the general principles that determine which of the variables will have its value fixed. How surprising this matter is, can best be illustrated by means of some examples.

Consider the following linear programming problem:

$$\text{Maximize:} \quad x_1 + x_4$$
$$\text{Subject to:} \quad x_1 - x_2 - x_3 \geqslant 0$$
$$x_1 \qquad\qquad \leqslant 10$$
$$x_1 \pm x_2 - x_4 \geqslant 0$$
$$x_3 \qquad\qquad \geqslant 5$$
$$x_i \geqslant 0 \quad \text{for all } i$$

The situation in the left-hand side of the third restriction determines whether all variables are fixed. If the third restriction has the plus sign, the four variables x_1, x_2, x_3 and x_4 have fixed values. If this restriction has the minus sign, the three variables x_1, x_2 and x_4 have fixed values, while x_3 can have any value between 5 and 10. It has been our experience that economic intuition often enabled us to predict whether a certain variable in a given model can be determined or not. It will be evident that it is difficult to base such a conclusion on the structure of the restrictions. The preceding set of restrictions can easily be triangularized, but this does not provide any insight as to the interdependence of the variables; thus, the beloved tool of input-output analysis is useless in the world of linear programming.

Closely analogous to the preceding result is the fact that the consequences of adding new restrictions to the model or the addition of new variables in the old and/or new restrictions, are difficult to analyse formally. We shall distinguish between five situations, which will be illustrated by means of examples. All the examples to be exhibited will be variations of the following problem for non-negative variables.

Schematic   Original Problem

——— Maximize: $x_1 + x_2$

Subject to: $x_1 + 2x_2 \leqslant 5$

$2x_1 + x_2 \leqslant 7$

The solution is $x_1 = 3$, $x_2 = 1$, which gives a maximum of 4 for the objective function.

Situation A: New restrictions are added in terms of the old variables.

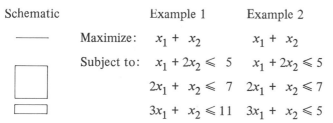

Schematic   Example 1   Example 2

——— Maximize: $x_1 + x_2$ $x_1 + x_2$

Subject to: $x_1 + 2x_2 \leqslant 5$ $x_1 + 2x_2 \leqslant 5$

$2x_1 + x_2 \leqslant 7$ $2x_1 + x_2 \leqslant 7$

$3x_1 + x_2 \leqslant 11$ $3x_1 + x_2 \leqslant 5$

This situation is a very transparent one. Either the original solution satisfies the new restriction, which leaves the optimum unaffected (Example 1), or the original solution violates the new restriction (Example 2), so that the solution has to be altered. The new optimum will have to be less favourable because the new optimal solution inevitably satisfies the old problem and cannot be more favourable than the old optimum one. In Example 2 the solution changes to $x_1 = 1$, $x_2 = 2$, with a maximum of the objective function of 3 instead of the original 4.

Situation B: New variables are introduced into the old restrictions.

Schematic   Example 1   Example 2

———

Maximize: $x_1 + x_2$ $x_1 + x_2$

Subject to: $x_1 + 2x_2 + x_3 \leqslant 5$ $x_1 + 2x_2 + x_3 \leqslant 5$

$2x_1 + x_2 + 2x_3 \leqslant 7$ $2x_1 + x_2 - 2x_3 \leqslant 7$

Example 3   Example 4

Maximize: $x_1 + x_2$ $x_1 + x_2$

Subject to: $x_1 + 2x_2 - x_3 \leqslant 5$ $x_1 + 2x_2 - x_3 \leqslant 5$

$2x_1 + x_2 + 2x_3 \leqslant 7$ $2x_1 + x_2 - 2x_3 \leqslant 7$

This situation is not trivial at all, except for Examples 1 and 4. In Example 1 the value of x_3 of course is set equal to 0 to attain the same optimum as in the original problem, and in Example 4 it is easily verified that the solution space is unbounded. But in the two remaining examples a new solution, preferable to the old one, might become possible. Actually this is the case in Example 2, where for the solution $x_1 = 17/4$, $x_2 = 0$, $x_3 = 3/4$, the objective function attains a slightly higher value than 4, whereas in Example 3 the old solution remains the optimal one. Now Example 4 will never occur in actual practise and the situation depicted by the Examples 2 and 3 will be exceptional because of the minus sign of the newly added variable in a "less than" inequality. In the normal case, therefore, the addition of new variables to the old restrictions will not alter the optimum because the new variables will be set equal to 0.

Situation C: New restrictions are added in terms of old and new variables.

Schematic   Example 1   Example 2

———

Maximize: $x_1 + x_2$ $x_1 + x_2$

Subject to: $x_1 + 2x_2 \quad\quad \leqslant 5$ $x_1 + 2x_2 \quad\quad \leqslant 5$

$2x_1 + x_2 \quad\quad \leqslant 7$ $2x_1 + x_2 \quad\quad \leqslant 7$

$3x_1 + x_2 + 2x_3 \leqslant 11$ $3x_1 + x_2 + 2x_3 \leqslant 5$

Example 3   Example 4

Maximize: $x_1 + x_2$ $x_1 + x_2$

Subject to: $x_1 + 2x_2 \quad\quad \leqslant 5$ $x_1 + 2x_2 \quad\quad \leqslant 5$

$2x_1 + x_2 \quad\quad \leqslant 7$ $2x_1 + x_2 \quad\quad \leqslant 7$

$3x_1 + x_2 - 2x_3 \leqslant 11$ $3x_1 + x_2 - 2x_3 \leqslant 5$

Examples 1 and 2 of this situation are completely equivalent to those in Situation A. In Example 1 the values of x_1 and x_2 are left unchanged, x_3 is undetermined between 0 and 1/2 and the optimum remains the same. In Example 2 the original solution does not satisfy the additional restriction so that a less favourable optimum must result. Example 3 also coincides with Example 1 of Situation A; the original solution satisfies the new restriction for all values of x_3, so the only interesting example is the fourth. Setting $x_3 > 1$ makes the third restriction not binding, implying that here also the optimum remains the same as the original one.

Situation D: New variables are introduced into old and new restrictions.

Schematic   Example 1   Example 2

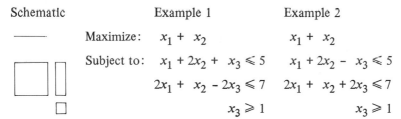

Maximize: $x_1 + x_2$ $x_1 + x_2$

Subject to: $x_1 + 2x_2 + x_3 \leqslant 5$ $x_1 + 2x_2 - x_3 \leqslant 5$

              $2x_1 + x_2 - 2x_3 \leqslant 7$ $2x_1 + x_2 + 2x_3 \leqslant 7$

                        $x_3 \geqslant 1$ $x_3 \geqslant 1$

This situation should be treated as a combination of Situations A and B. First the possibilities according to Situation B (thus for the old restrictions) are analysed, resulting in the same or a higher optimum. Then the (new) solution is checked for the new restriction according to Situation A. As has been stated, new restrictions can never improve the optimum; at most, it remains unaffected. Combining Situations A and B gives rise to at least eight combinations, most of which, however, are not very interesting. In Example 1 the optimal solution for the first two restrictions was $x_1 = 17/4, x_2 = 0, x_3 = 3/4$. This solution, however, does not satisfy $x_3 \geqslant 1$. Thus, the third restriction becomes binding as well and a new solution has to be found. One finds $x_1 = 4, x_2 = 0, x_3 = 1$. The value of the objective has decreased by 1/4 to 4. In Example 2 the optimal solution for the first two restrictions was the original solution with x_3 set equal to 0. This solution does not satisfy $x_3 \geqslant 1$; thus, the optimum has to decrease. The new solution is $x_1 = 4/3, x_2 = 7/3, x_3 = 1$, with all restrictions binding. The value of the objective has decreased by 1/3.

Situation E: New variables are introduced and new restrictions are added. This situation is to be treated exactly like Situation D. The incorporation of new variables in the original restrictions might be beneficial for the optimum and is never harmful. The addition of new restrictions (in all variables) might be quite harmful and is never beneficial. On mathematical grounds, the final result is not to be predicted. On economic arguments, we dare to venture that in Situation E the optimum will never rise.

As already mentioned earlier in this section, the MPSX/370 package contains facilities to revise a problem in many ways and to start the solution of the revised problem in a fashion that suits the circumstances. This together with the feature that enables the user to unload a problem file onto a sequentially organised storage device (generally tape), makes the actual execution of the computations discussed in this chapter a simple task for anyone who desires to perform similar calculations on the basis of the same description of production and capital formation.

3 TWO VERSIONS
OF THE MODEL
The Choice of a Period
for Optimization

3.1 INTRODUCTION

The model as it is presented in the preceding chapter, has been written in a dynamic form in the sense that all vectors of variables have been given a time index. As soon as one wants to perform any computations, a choice has to be made about the length of the period over which the target function is to be optimized. There is an essential difference between optimization over a 1-year period and optimization over a more-than-1-year period, regarding the way the system behaves. If optimization takes place over a period of 2 years or more, investments in the first year play an important role because they help to build the production capacity for future years. Optimizing over several years, the investment decisions (the choice between investing and consuming) on the one hand, and the allocation of investments over the sectors on the other hand, will be implied by the model. Investments as well as all other variables are in general completely determined in the LP-solution, except those for the last year in the sequence, in which no choice can be made between increase of production capacity or consumption as final destination of the investment goods. In that last year the system has become completely myopic. It has no horizon, no future to provide for and to take into consideration. Similarly, if one optimizes over a

1-year period, this one particular year is the last year and the LP-solution fails to determine investments. Therefore in successive 1-year optimizations, the investment decisions have to be made separately in one way or another. We shall discuss this problem in the next section.

Thus, the choice between a time horizon of 1 year and a time horizon of several years entails two essentially different versions of the model. We investigated both of them. To gain some experience with the behaviour of the system, we started analysing a test model consisting of four sectors only. The results for this test model are presented and discussed in Chapter 5, those for the full 22-sector model are discussed in Chapter 6. The results for the test model with successive year-to-year optimizations were so poor that we decided not to perform this kind of optimization with the full model; therefore, in Chapter 6 only results of the more-years optimization are analysed. Because of its interesting theoretical aspects, however, we treat the year-to-year optimization technique in rather great detail in the next section.

3.2 YEAR-TO-YEAR OPTIMIZATION

Aggregation into a Four-Sector Test Model

Actual computations for the year-to-year optimizations were started with a test model that consisted of four sectors. Each sector was obtained by aggregating sectors of the 22-sector model.[1] We hasten to emphasize that this super aggregation was not intended to produce the conventional four-sector model consisting of the aggregates agriculture, industry, services and government. The rationale for our way of aggregation was the necessity to have two sectors that deliver investment goods apart from consumption goods, two being the minimum that is required to test the behaviour of the system in several modifications of the model. We further needed the pollution abatement activity as a separate sector and one conventional sector that solely delivers goods for consumption purposes. Finally, we tried to aggregate in such a way that actual production of the three conventional sectors has about the same value. These considerations led to the following classification:

Sector 1: among other sectors: Building and Commerce
Sector 2: among other sectors: Chemical Products, Metal Products and Means of Transport
Sector 3: Agriculture, Foods, Textiles and the services sectors (exclusive of Commerce)
Sector 4: All abatement sectors

It is useless to try and find unambiguous names for these sectors; aggregation brought birds of too different a feather in one nest together. A rough nomenclature might be: 1 building; 2 heavy industry; 3 consumption industry; 4 pollution abatement. Note also that we made a minor change in the numerical data of the model by setting the export surplus equal to 0 in each sector. Because of the extreme extent of aggregation, this assumption is not far beyond the truth and it simplifies the model somewhat.

A Separate (Sub)model for the Investment Decisions

Given a minimum level for each good's consumption and a maximum level for the production in each sector, the normal situation will be that actual production exceeds the needs for intermediate deliveries plus the minimal requirement for consumption. Thus in general there will be a production surplus, which can be expressed as a "slack" in the Leontief restriction. For sectors that only deliver consumption goods, the slack can be allocated to consumption or export. For sectors that deliver investment goods, the slack can also be used for expansion of the productive capacity. If both sectors that deliver investment goods have a slack, expansion of the productive capacity in one or more sectors becomes possible.

Under more-years optimization, the incentive to invest is provided by the objective function, because investments in a given year tend to increase the contribution to the value of the objective function of future years. It will be profitable to direct investments towards those sectors for which this increase is the largest.

In a model with a 1-year optimization period, the objective function cannot perform this task. Only 1 year is taken into consideration, and therefore the objective function is indifferent with respect to the choice between consumption and investment. A completely different approach to determine investments is needed. To this end we introduce two kinds of decision makers, the entrepreneurs and the investors. The entrepreneurs decide how much to produce in each sector. This decision process constitutes the production model. The investors decide how to allocate the available slacks. The way in which this is done is described in an investment model.

At the beginning of each year the entrepreneurs allocate production capacity to optimize the objective function, taking into account the existing restrictions. This production plan, together with the appropriate shadow prices, is the point of departure for the investors, who decide to invest in those sectors where the shadow prices on the capacity restrictions are highest. Of course, investments cannot surpass the available slacks.

Both sets of decisions are then put into operation. Referring to Section 1.5, it is assumed that the time span in which investment decisions are converted into capital stock equals 1 year, so that at the beginning of the next year these investments are part of existing capacity and the same process can be put into operation at the beginning of that next year. Schematically this procedure can be visualized as follows:

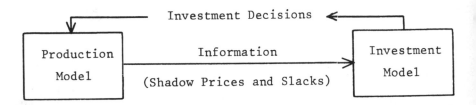

The concept of shadow prices is well known in the context of linear programming. In mathematical parlance they are called *Lagrange multipliers.* Their economic interpretation is that they represent the increase in value of the objective function, if the amount of a scarce resource (in our case existing capacity) would be increased by one unit. They are thus a measure of the severity of a restriction and the general idea is therefore to invest in those sectors where scarcity is most pronounced.

The idea of using shadow prices to control investments is of course not a new one. Tj.C. Koopmans[2] uses shadow prices for the attainment of efficiency under a regime of decentralized decisions. Ginsburgh and Waelbroek[3] state: ". . . shadowprices of capital, labour and foreign exchange which are then interpreted as approximations of what equilibrium prices would be, if markets for these commodities were competitive. . .". We can translate these arguments into formulae as follows. Denoting the vector of wage shares in the objective function by ξ, the vector of slacks in the Leontief restrictions by s_t and all other symbols as defined in Section 2.2, the production model for the year t can be written as:

Objective Function: Maximize $\xi' x_t$ (all sectors regarded)

Leontief Restrictions,

   conventional sectors: $(I - A_{11} - D_{11}) x_{ct} - (A_{12} + D_{12}) x_{at} - f_{c(t-1)} = s_{ct}$

   abatement sectors: $(I - A_{22}) x_{at} - A_{21} x_{ct} + (I - H) f_{a(t-1)} = s_{at}$

Capacity Restrictions: $x_t \leqslant w_t$

In this formulation the political restrictions are substituted into the corresponding Leontief restrictions. For the conventional sectors these political restrictions imply that the consumption in year t at least equals consumption in year $t - 1$. For the abatement sectors the elements of the diagonal matrix $\mathbf{H}$ are positive fractions, representing the required annual rate of decrease of admitted nuisance. The elements of $\mathbf{w}_t$—the capacities at the beginning of year t—are given constants, as are the elements of $\mathbf{f}_{t-1}$. The production levels $\mathbf{x}_t$ and the slacks $\mathbf{s}_t$ are solved by this LP-problem, while the simplex algorithm also provides the vectors of shadow prices. Only those on the capacity restrictions are needed in the sequel and their vector is denoted by $\mathbf{p}_t$.

The investment model then runs as follows:

Objective Function: Maximize $\mathbf{p}_t'\mathbf{y}_t$ (all sectors regarded)

Restrictions: $\mathbf{K}\mathbf{y}_t \leqslant \mathbf{s}_{ct}$

This model yields the vector $\mathbf{y}_t$ of expansions of production capacity. Once this vector is known, consumption in year t and capacity at the beginning of next year are known:

$$\mathbf{f}_{ct} = \mathbf{f}_{c(t-1)} + \mathbf{s}_{ct} - \mathbf{K}\mathbf{y}_t$$

$$\mathbf{f}_{at} = (\mathbf{I} - \mathbf{H})\,\mathbf{f}_{a(t-1)} - \mathbf{s}_{at} \quad \text{(by definition)}$$

$$\mathbf{w}_{t+1} = \mathbf{w}_t + \mathbf{y}_t$$

Now all data needed for the computations for the year $t + 1$ are available, so that these computations can be performed for that particular year. It is a lemma in LP-theory that the number of nonzero activities in the optimum solution of a problem in standard format will in general not exceed the number of inequality restrictions. This implies that the number of sectors in which production capacity will be increased, will not exceed the number of sectors that deliver investment goods. Because the latter number is less than the number of sectors, it is to be predicted that expansion of production capacity each year will be concentrated in a few sectors.

It is sometimes possible to escape from these unrealistic time paths of sectoral capacities. Shadow prices remain constant within a certain range of widening the restrictions. They change abruptly the moment another restriction becomes binding. This suggests that the shadow prices only remain constant over a limited range of expanding the capacities. The output of the MPSX/370 package contains the values of these limits, so that it is technically quite easy to restrict investments within these limits. With the incorporation of these limits as additional restrictions, the number of sectors in which capacity is expanded might rise. We are aware that this procedure is a highly artificial one. For if one realises that investment decisions are taken according to present opportunity by individual decision makers, how can any of them know a range condition is met? In our opinion, the answer to this question is not obvious. Nevertheless, the range conditions were incorporated in the investment model to achieve a better performance of the system.

Preliminary Adjustments in Year-to-Year Optimization

It turned out that it was not easy at all to find a feasible path for the system in the successive 1-year optimizations, not even with range conditions taken into account. Emergency measures had to be taken before such a path could be found. The first alteration of the original production model was the reduction of the rate of decrease for admitted nuisance from 10 percent to 5 percent annually, in combination with the incorporation of enforced investments in the abatement sector. The decrease in admitted nuisance necessitates an increase in the production capacity of the pollution abatement sector. In a given year the system does not know that next year it has to provide for this contingency, which leads to poor performance. Therefore, we added a restriction that forces the system to build the pollution abatement capacity necessary to meet next year's requirements. The enforced investments in the abatement sector are a natural and necessary redress of the myopia of the system.

With this modification, the system did survive for a year or two, but then another problem arose. Because all slacks that are not invested are added to final consumption and consumption in the next year is at least equal to consumption in this year, the system became infeasible because consumption increased too fast. The system could not permanently afford these extras. To avoid this kind of difficulty we incorporated in the model a 50-percent habituation ratio for consumption. By this is meant that in each sector the minimal level of consumption for next year equals this year's minimal consumption plus one half of this year's supplementary consumption.

After this modification it became possible to run the model for a number of years. The objective function, the sum of wages, could increase at the modest growth rate of 2 percent annually during the first 5 years. After the fifth year the system became stabilized; no more investments, no more growth. We may refer to Chapter 5 for the presentation of the detailed results.

An Alternative (Sub)model for the Investment Decisions

The investment submodel as presented in this section so far, is of course only one out of various possibilities to solve the problem of investments in the case of successive 1-year optimizations. Though the use of shadow prices as described in the investment model finds theoretical support, other solutions can be considered. The investment model in its original form has some disadvantages that are easily foreseen. One of these is that a high shadow price on the capacity of a sector that is of minor economic importance, will lead to relatively enormous investments in that sector, thus steering the system away from balanced growth. Another disadvantage has already been mentioned, namely, the irregularity of the yearly expansion of the capacities. One would prefer a smoother movement of investments in time, permitting (some) continuous growth, especially in a model that is so very myopic.

These disadvantages can be overcome by using the economic importance of the sectors, as well as the shadow prices, in directing investments. To this end, we made the increase in the production capacity of a sector proportional to the product of its shadow price and the existing production capacity:

$$y_{jt} = \lambda_t \, p_{jt} \, w_{jt} \qquad \text{for all } j$$

In other words, the shadow prices determine the relative increase of capacity instead of the absolute one. The multiplicator λ will be chosen as large as possible, with respect to the availability restrictions on the investment goods, derived from the solution of the production model:

$$\mathbf{K} y_t \leqslant s_t$$

Doing so, one kills two birds with one stone. If a sector produces below its capacity, just as before, no investments in that sector take place because the shadow price will be 0. In the other case, with production at full capacity, the economic importance of the sectors also influences the investment decisions.

To find λ, as well as the y_j's, it is not necessary anymore to solve an LP-problem. Omitting the time index, the following restriction for the ith investment good holds:

$$\sum_j k_{ij} y_j \leqslant s_i$$

or:

$$\lambda \sum_j k_{ij} p_j w_j \leqslant s_i$$

so that:

$$\lambda = \min_i \frac{s_i}{\sum_j k_{ij} p_j w_j}$$

We can see that λ is chosen in such a way that (at least) one of the slacks from the production LP-problem is just exhausted, which implies that λ is as large as possible.

This revised submodel for the investment decisions has a certain robustness towards disaggregation of sectors. If the shadow prices of the production capacities of two sectors are equal, investment behaviour outside these sectors is the same whether or not the two sectors are aggregated. This is of some importance because the calculations were only performed for the test model.

In this alternative version of the investment model, the range conditions have to be omitted because they contradict the principle of proportionality. Enforced investments in the abatement sector and the habituation ratio of one-half for consumption were retained, however.

It worked out that the performance of the system was more balanced than in the former case. A continuing (modest) growth at a rate of 1.5 percent annually became attainable. Again, we refer to Chapter 5 for the detailed results.

3.3 A 10-YEAR PERIOD OF OPTIMIZATION

The Period of Optimization

The moment it is decided that optimization will be performed over a period of more than 1 year, several questions arise that have to be answered in advance. The main question, of course, regards the precise length of the period. A distinction must be made between the number of years we want to look ahead (the length of the *period of interest*) and the length of the *period of optimization*. The period of optimization (to be denoted by T) has to be chosen somewhat longer than the period of interest (to be denoted by θ), because when taking T equal to θ, one again gets mixed up with the problem of myopia. This is because in the year T itself the system is completely deprived of a future to provide for and therefore may behave quite nonsensically. In this context one should keep in mind that the aim of this study is to investigate the realizability of socioeconomic desiderata. Whereas most of these desiderata pertain to the near future, our main interest lies in the performance of the system over not too long a period.

It will be intuitively clear that the greater the time span becomes over which the optimization is sought, the more roundabout ways of production will become profitable. Increasing the production capacity of a sector in which excess capacity already exists can hardly be profitable in the short run. If one takes a longer point of view it might, however, become advantageous. This implies that the time series for the variables generated by the system, in general, will change if the length of the period of optimization is changed from T to $T + 1$ years. But for the first θ years in the sequence these changes may become small if T is sufficiently larger than θ. We therefore should like to choose T large enough, so that the behaviour of the time series over a time span θ becomes stable, in other words, does not change anymore if T is increased.

By experimenting with the model for a given θ, one could obtain an estimate of the required T. This was not done systematically. We have chosen a period of optimization of 10 years, which was considered to be sufficient for a period of interest of 7 years,[4] the same period of interest as that used in the Dutch government publication mentioned in Section 2.1.

The Discount Rate

There are some more questions to be answered. The first one is whether the objective function should be written as the unweighted sum of total wages or that a weighted sum should be taken, with weights geometrically approaching 0 with time. In the latter case, a value for the ratio of the series of weights must be chosen as well. Occasionally in optimizing practise, arguments are expressed in favour of such a rate of discount. One argument holds that, even in the absence of uncertainty, individuals will judge a unit of consumption tomorrow less attractive than that same physical unit of consumption today. This problem of time preference is a very involved one indeed. We may refer to Chakravarty for a discussion.[5] It is our opinion that the argument holds less for societies than for individuals.

Another argument starts from the increasing uncertainty in time regarding the constancy of all kinds of properties of the system. Of course we do not deny this aspect, but we do not believe that discounting the objective function is the best way to deal with it. As stated in Section 2.4, the way to deal with uncertainty in this context is to introduce different scenarios and to perform sensitivity analyses.

A final argument in favour of discounting the future in dynamic models is that if discounting is neglected, the generated time series sometimes will show characteristics that are not realistic in actual planning practise. Our model, for instance, sometimes invests in a sector in which excess capacity already exists because that is advantageous in the long run. Discounting will tend to avert this kind of behaviour, but it is fascinating to observe the time paths of the variables that the system constructs to conquer its obstacles. Therefore, we thought it best not to make the system less perceptive by introducing a discount rate.

Terminal Conditions

Terminal conditions are an essential element in dynamic optimization literature, where their practical as well as their theoretical aspects are extensively dealt with.

Incorporation of terminal conditions becomes necessary if one wishes to consider parts of the postplan future into the model. The theoretical aspects find their origin in the fact that the terminal conditions are expressed as equalities, which make it possible by means of differentiating to investigate the sensitivity of the optimal value of the objective function to a change in the terminal conditions.

The formulation of restrictions as equalities is contrary to our philosophy professed in Section 2.1, while the considerations which led us to a terminal time of 10 years have been presented in this section. We thus feel that if we should have to introduce terminal conditions, we should formulate them as inequalities. However, the discussion on the choice of the period of optimization will have made it obvious that the introduction of terminal conditions that prevent senseless behaviour of the time series towards the end of the period of interest, is more or less superfluous.

The Structure of the LP Problem

A few remarks might be spent on the structure of the LP-problem in the 10-year optimization version. The model as it has been presented in Section 2.2 consists of 88 restrictions, besides the nonnegative ones. For each of the 22 sectors there was a Leontief restriction, a capacity restriction, a disinvestment restriction and a political restriction. As the time index t runs from 1 to 10, we end up with an LP-problem with 880 restrictions.

In the Leontief restrictions the dynamic element is introduced in the definition of investments, which constitute the increase in production capacity of year t to year $t + 1$. The capacity in year 1 is an initial condition to the model. The disinvestment restrictions $w_{t+1} \geqslant w_t$ and the political restrictions:

$$f_{it} \geqslant f_{i(t-1)} \qquad (i = 1, \ldots, 17)$$
$$f_{it} \leqslant (1 - \phi)f_{i(t-1)} \qquad (i = 18, \ldots, 22)$$

also link variables with different time indices.

It is instructive to present the structure of the LP-problem in a diagrammatic form, as has been done in Table 3.3.1. To characterize the typical structure of this LP-problem, one might say it has an (imperfect) block-diagonal one. Each block contains variables dated $t - 1$, t and $t + 1$. Overlap only enters for two adjoining years. Because of this structure the *density* of the coefficient matrix is very low; actually, it is only half a percent. It goes without saying that this typical structure of the system leads to a considerable reduction in computing time, which is worthwhile because the model has almost 900 restrictions in about 700 variables.

Table 3.3.1. Structure of the LP-Problem in 10-Year Optimization.

Type of Restrictions	Initial Conditions			Time-Indexed Variables								
	h_0	w_1	f_0	x_1	w_2	f_1	x_2	w_3	f_2	x_3	w_4	f_3
Year 1 Leontief	x	x		x	x	x						
Capacity		x		x								
Disinvestment		x			x							
Political			x			x						
Year 2 Leontief	x				x		x	x	x			
Capacity					x		x					
Disinvestment					x			x				
Political						x			x			
Year 3 Leontief	x							x		x	x	x
Capacity								x		x		
Disinvestment								x			x	
Political									x			x

Some Additional Restrictions

As has been said in the introduction to this chapter, computations were started with a four-sector test model. The performance of this test model in the 10-year optimization was so promising that we started at once with computations on the full 22-sector model. Chapter 6 will show in detail that the full model in the form presented thus far has many opportunities for growth. The annual wage sum in the period of interest is increasing at an average rate of 17 percent, thus leading to the conclusion that the requirements regarding pollution abatement can be realised without too many difficulties. Of course the rise in the annual wage sum, which is astonishingly high, is the theoretical maximum that can be attained. To this end, the LP-solution has searched in an ingenious way for the most advantageous time paths of investments—investing particularly in sectors with low capital coefficients. In reality, this would imply a very stringent planning of annual investments in the 22 sectors and we are aware of the fact that this is hardly possible. Only a result far below the computed maximum will be attainable. Nevertheless, we state that pollution abatement together with the modest desiderata introduced thus far is realizable if investments are carefully planned.

Examining the performance of the model in more detail, we noticed that in some sectors growth was so exorbitant that one is forced to reconsider the basic assumptions. In particular, the system is extremely reluctant to allocate goods for consumption purposes. The increase in consumption is delayed to the last year(s) of the period of optimization and is completely missing in the period of interest. This, of course, is a consequence of the system's endeavour to increase the total wage sum as much as possible. Investment does serve this objective, while an increase of consumption leaves the objective function unchanged.

The combination of the two results, abundant growth of production and restrained consumption, certainly must be considered very unrealistic in democratic societies. Why should people earn more income and not spend it on more (conventional) goods? Even if labour is not scarce, a necessary condition for excessive growth, it remains a must that conventional consumption increases at about the same rate as the wage sum. This consideration led us to add an additional restriction to the model. This restriction will be called the *consumption-proportionality restriction*. It compels total consumption to grow each year at least at the same rate as the wage sum. In the symbols of the model this is written as:

$$\sum_{i=1}^{17} f_{it} \geqslant \rho \sum_{i=1}^{22} \xi_i x_{it} \qquad (t = 1, \ldots, 10)$$

where ρ can be treated as a parameter or can be determined by the initial conditions of the model, which was our procedure. The newly added restriction will prove to be of great importance for the performance of the system and the value of the optimum. The average annual growth rate of the wage sum declines to about 9 percent. It should be emphasized that the system retains its freedom to select which goods and what amounts are to be consumed. The amounts are subject to the political restrictions on conventional consumption and, of course, to the newly added proportionality restriction. As will be shown in Chapter 6, the system uses this freedom in quite a peculiar way. It is mainly the sector Commerce which delivers the additional consumption; people have to consume much more in the way of trade services.

Even with the consumption-proportionality restriction taken into account, the production growth in some sectors remains enormous, with annual rates of growth far above 20 percent. Although it is very difficult to pinpoint limits to annual growth of production capacity for a sector, there must be some. The obvious way to achieve a restraining of excessive growth rates, simply is to put an upper limit on them. To get some insight into the implications of this adaptation of the model, a run was made in which the production capacity of all sectors was not allowed to increase more than 10 percent annually. Written in the symbols of the model, the capacity restrictions were changed into:

$$w_{t-1} \leqslant w_t \leqslant 1{,}1 \, w_{t-1}$$

The way to achieve more balance in the system, is a further curtailment of its freedom to select which goods are to be consumed. This can be realised by enforcing balanced growth of consumption—in other words, consumption of all goods should increase at a given rate at least. To that end, the political restrictions on conventional consumption were changed into:

$$f_{it} \geqslant (1 + \phi) f_{i(t-1)} \qquad (i = 1, \ldots, 17)$$

Some values of ϕ were tested. The system could support a value of ϕ equal to 1 percent, but when ϕ is equal to 2 percent the system becomes infeasible. In other words, 2 percent balanced growth in conventional consumption together with 10 percent decrease in admitted nuisance, cannot be realised. However, if the consumption of Sector XVI (the sector incorporating the branch "leasing of movables and real estate") is excluded from this last set of political restrictions, the joint ϕ for all other goods may reach a much higher value. Of course, this modification is in conflict with the balanced growth idea.

Finally, there are the possibilities of restricting growth in certain sectors in view of the scarcity of raw materials and energy. As an example, a run is made in which the production capacity in the Energy sector is allowed to increase every year with 2 percent only. More or less to our surprise, the system could bear this burden, but of course the rate of growth of the wage sum became very modest.

3.4 LONG-TERM VERSUS SHORT-TERM OPTIMIZATION

In this chapter, two essentially different versions of our model were discussed, a long-term version with a period of optimization of 10 years and a short-term version where optimization is performed over a sequence of successive 1-year periods.

The fundamental difference between the two versions is that for the 10-year optimization we do not need an explicit theory of investments. The system itself directs investments in such a fashion that the objective function is maximized. In the version that optimizes over a sequence of successive 1-year periods, the objective function for a given year does not reflect the results of the investment policy in that year, because the resulting increase of production capacity becomes available during later years. An explicit theory directing investments thus becomes necessary. We have decided to test a theory that is not very common in economics—a liberty that seems permissible in the light of the lack of a communis opinio regarding investment theory—but which fits well within the environment of a linear programming model and which cannot be denied a certain intuitive plausibility. According to this theory, investments are directed to those sectors where the scarcity of capital goods—as measured by the shadow price on the capacity restriction—is greatest.

Both versions have their pros and cons. The 1-year version is perhaps preferable, because it is the most realistic one in the sense that it approaches reality better than the 10-year version. Individual decision makers will not plan too far into the future because they are faced with uncertainty, and therefore short-term arguments would be decisive. An overwhelming practical objection against this version, however, is that it does not work; the system is not capable of satisfying the requirements regarding growth, pollution abatement and the increase of consumption, that are customarily thought to be essential. This version of the model suffers from a shortcoming that we have called myopia. This is caused by the fact that shadow prices only reflect the scarcity as it exists at a given moment of time. The system is not capable of taking into account the consequences of actions taken at that time, as far as the effects come to light at a later date. Striking examples of this myopia—which shadow prices may have in common with the actual market prices—will be given later on. We have investigated the year-to-year optimization version only by means of a highly aggregated 4-sector test model, the idea originally being to perform the calculations also for the full 22-sector model. We decided to omit the last step because of the poor performance of the test model. We will describe and analyse our experiments with the test model in detail in Chapter 5, where we will show how we had to alleviate the requirements in order to keep the system alive during 10 successive years. As the role of prices in dynamic economic theory is rather obscure, we believe that our analysis raises legitimate questions regarding the suitability of the price mechanism as a steering device under dynamic circumstances.

The 10-year optimization version did not exhibit any of those difficulties. The system gives the impression of being very robust. It can support a reasonable rate of growth together with fulfilment of the many additional requirements that a modern society might demand of its productive apparatus. The main and only question is how realistic this model is. If one follows the time paths of the variables, it becomes immediately obvious that the investment policy adopted is a very sophisticated one. We shall demonstrate this trait extensively in Chapter 6. The conclusion will inevitably be that one cannot expect a democratic society — with its many frictions—to be so efficient that it will be capable of matching the performance of the system. The results of the computations have to be viewed as the absolute maximum that is attainable under the postulated circumstances, a warning that becomes even more severe, if one keeps in mind that the omission of behavourial restrictions also tends to an overestimation of the maximum of the objective function. What might be realisable in reality, might be much less than is suggested by the performance of the system under 10-year optimization.

II EMPIRICAL INVESTIGATIONS

4 STATISTICAL RESEARCH

4.1 FACTOR ANALYSIS OF TECHNOLOGY MATRICES

In Section 1.2 a factor analytic model was presented that was devised to find an aggregation key for the 56 branches of the 1965 input-output tables. The method of principal components, followed by the well-known varimax rotation, yields a matrix of so-called *factor loadings,* the elements of which can be interpreted as the weights of the (observed) technologies on the (nonobserved) basic technologies. Our main interest is focussed on this matrix of factor loadings, but we have not yet indicated how to fix the order of this matrix.

In applications of the method of principal components, the number of common factors and therefore the number of basic technologies, is often taken as the number of eigenvalues of the correlation matrix that are greater than 1. The rationale for this "stoprule" can be explained as follows. If W is the diagonal matrix of the M largest eigenvalues of the correlation matrix R and Q is the (m by M) matrix of corresponding orthonormal eigenvectors (thus, $Q'Q = I$), then the principal component solution for the matrix of factor loadings (L) is written as:

$$L = W^{1/2} Q'$$

According to the factor analytic model, the correlation matrix **R** is approximately reproduced by the matrix product $\mathbf{L'L}$.[1] Now tr $(\mathbf{L'L})$ = tr $(\mathbf{LL'})$ = tr $(\mathbf{W})$. As tr $(\mathbf{R})$ equals the summation of m ones (1s), it will be clear that the contribution to the explanation of the total variation of the (standardized) variables of an additional factor with an eigenvalue smaller than 1, is less than the contribution of such a variable itself.

Our computational work started with a factor analysis of the columns of the 1965 input-output matrix for the European Economic Community,[2] using the stoprule mentioned. This resulted in 15 factors, with an index of factorization of 88.[3] This number of factors is rather close to 17, the number of aggregates that has been used by the SOEC.

To "scale" this result, that is, to investigate whether the branches could be considered to belong to definite sectors, we performed the same analysis on a matrix with elements consisting of random drawings from an exponential distribution with parameter .01. This distribution and this particular value of its parameter were chosen to obtain numbers comparable to the observed technical coefficients. Here we found 23 factors with an index of factorization of 83, while the first 15 had an index of only 66. Although there is quite a difference between the results of both analyses, it is still too early to conclude that factor analysis is a powerful method for aggregation purposes. To investigate this, we first examine the factor loadings after the varimax rotation.

The aim of the varimax rotation is to obtain for every variable (i.e., every column) a large loading on only one factor and small loadings on all the other factors. There exists no significance test for rotated loadings. However, if a factor loading is seen as a correlation coefficient between a variable and a factor, the standard error $1/\sqrt{m}$ of a zero correlation (for normally distributed variables) can be used as a rough indication of its standard error. Since $m = 55$ in this analysis,[4] $1/\sqrt{m}$ is about .15; thus, the level of significance for a factor loading is about .3. A factor loading of .3 accounts for a little less than 10 percent of the variation of a variable. A more important critical value is .7, because this value implies that one-half of the variation of a variable is accounted for by one factor and, moreover, that no loading on any other factor can reach the same size; thus such a variable can be classified unambiguously.

At this moment it might be useful to present a point of some subtlety. The method of factor analysis provides us with factor loadings on 15 factors to be interpreted as weights on basic technologies. By looking at these factor loadings we try to classify branches into sectors in such a way that each branch belongs to one and only one sector. The moment we possess such a classification scheme, aggregation of the input-output matrices from the branch level to the sector level is straightforward. By dividing the elements of the aggregated input-output matrix by the corresponding aggregated amounts of actual production, the aggregated technology matrix is obtained. One should not expect that the columns of this technology matrix—after standardization—will exactly equal the (columns of the) factors resulting from the factor analysis—after rowwise aggregation—but if the factor analysis has been successful, there will be a close resemblance. In the sequel, therefore, we will not consider the difference between factors and sectors to be significant and shall designate both by the same names. For reasons of convenience we shall "invent" those names by looking mainly at the kind of output of the branches classified into that sector. To distinguish between sectors/factors and branches/variables we shall systematically denote the former with a capital letter and the latter in lowercase.

The 15 factors in order of their contribution to the index of factorization are:

1. Foods
2. Instruments
3. Chemistry and Medicines
4. Metals
5. Petro
6. Textiles
7. Building
8. Administration
9. Mining
10. Paper
11. Leather Goods
12. Automobiles
13. Nonferrous
14. Money Affairs
15. Catering

The naming of the fifth factor will be explained in due course. All the other names describe outputs.

Of the 55 branches (listed in Table 4.1.1), 41 can be uniquely classified because of a factor loading over .7 and what's more, on each of the 15 factors we find at least one such a loading so that each factor may indeed be associated with a basic technology.

Each of the remaining 14 branches has at least one factor loading over .3, but most of them have two or three significant loadings. It is fully understandable that some branches are significantly related to more than one factor. It merely indicates that the input structure of such a branch really is of a mixed character. The most obvious method to relate each of these 14 branches to one single factor still seems to be according to their highest loading. For the variables 9, 10, 11, 17 and 52, with one loading of order .6 and the other significant loading(s) of order .4, this is still rather satisfactory.[5] For the remaining nine variables any classification is in fact arbitrary.

Table 4.1.2 is constructed according to this method of classification. The sectors (columns in this table) are ordered according to their contribution to the index of factorization. The branches (rows in this table) are—within each sector—listed according to the sequence in Table 4.1.1. A double plus sign (++) represents a factor loading over .7; a single plus sign (+) represents a factor loading over .3.

Table 4.1.1.   List of Branches.

Branch Number	SOEC Sector	Brief Description
1	I	Agriculture
2	I	Fishing
3	II	Coal lignite, briquettes and coke
4	II	Crude petroleum, natural gas and refined products
5	II	Electric power, distribution of gas, water, etc.
6	III	Iron and nonferrous ores
7	III	Blast furnace products
8	III	Nonferrous metals
9	IV	Bricks, ceramics
10	IV	Cement
11	IV	Glass
12	V	Chemical and plastic products
13	VI	Foundry products
14	VI	Other metal structures
15	VI	Agricultural and industrial machinery, etc.
16	VI	Electronic computers and office machines
17	VI	Electrical equipment
18	VII	Motor vehicles
19	VII	Ship building
20	VII	Motorcycles, bicycles
21	VI	Precision instruments
22	VIII	Animal or vegetable fats
23	VIII	Meats, etc.
24	VIII	Milk and dairy products
25	VIII	Preserved fruit, vegetables and fish
26	VIII	Cereal products
27	VIII	Sugar
28	VIII	Cacao, chocolate and sugar-confectionery products
29	VIII	Animal feeding products
30	VIII	Miscellaneous products for human consumption
31	VIII	Beverages
32	VIII	Tobacco products
33	IX	Textile products
34	IX	Hides and skins
35	IX	Leather goods other than footwear
36	IX	Footwear
37	IX	Clothing and fur goods
38	XI	Timber and wooden products
39	X	Paper and paper articles
40	X	Products of the printing, press and publishing trade
41	XI	Rubber products

Table 4.1.1. (Continued)

Branch Number	SOEC Sector	Brief Description
42	XI	Products of miscellaneous industries
43	XII	Construction of building and civil engineering works
44	XIII	Recovery and reuse
45	XIII	Wholesale and retail trade
46	XIII	Lodging and catering services
47	XIII	Repairs to motor vehicles, etc.
48	XIII	Repairs not otherwise specified
49	XIV	Transport services, etc.
50	XV	Financial and insurance services
51	XVI	Leasing of movables and real estate
52	XVI	Educational and scientific research services
53	XVI	Health services
54	XVII	General administrative services of public administration
55	XVII	Administrative services otherwise
56	XVII	Domestic services

For most branches within the same sector, economic and/or technical arguments can be used to explain why their input structures are similar. There is some tendency towards vertical integration of branches. The agriculture (1) branch is in the Foods sector and the repairs to motor vehicles (47) branch is in the Automobiles sector. The sector named Petro contains the refinery (4) and transport services (49) branches as well. Here it will be clear that "Petro" is a code for input similarity; both branches mentioned are notable users of liquid energy. The position of fishing (2) as a mixture of Petro and Textiles is not surprising, nor the position of wholesale and retail trade (45) as a mixture of Petro and Money Affairs. The construction industry (43) belongs to Building and so do the brick industry (9) and the cement industry (10). The branch timber (38), that might be supposed to belong to Building as well, does so only in a very marginal way.

It might be expected that the communality (i.e., the part of the variance described by all common factors) for the 14 "problem" variables is relatively low. However, this is only true for the variables 2, 6, 17, 34, 38, 42 and 55, and among these variables only the communalities of 34, 38 and 55 are (in this order) lower than the smallest communality of the 41 well-to-be classified variables. This justifies the classification of the other 11 variables into one of the 15 aggregates. On the other hand, it might be better to treat hides (34) and timber (38) as belonging to factors that did not yet manifest themselves. In the 15-

72 EMPIRICAL INVESTIGATIONS

Table 4.1.2. Classification after a Factor Analysis with 15 Extracted Factors.

Branch/ Variable	Sector/Factor														
	1	2	3	4	5	6	7	8	9	10	11	12	13	14	15
1	++														
22	++														
23	++														
24	++														
25	++														
26	++														
27	++														
28	++														
29	++														
30	++														
31	++														
32	++														+
6		+	+						+						
15		++		+											
16		++													
17		+											+		
21		++											+		
48		+				+									
11			+		+		+								
12			++												
41			++												
42			+										+		
53			++		+			+							
7				++											
13				++			+						+		
14				++											
19		+		++											
20		+		++											
2					+	+									
4					++										
45					+					+				+	
49					++										
33						++									
37						++									
9			+		+		+								
10					+		+		+						
38	+						+								
43		+					++								

Table 4.1.2. (Continued)

Branch/ Variable	Sector/Factor														
	1	2	3	4	5	6	7	8	9	10	11	12	13	14	15
51								++							
52			+		+			+							
54		+						++							
3									++						
5					+				++						
39										++					
40										++					
34											+				
35											++				
36											++				
18												++			
47												++			
8													++		
44		+												+	
50														++	
55					+			+						+	
46															++

factor solution they do not really fit. For a miscellaneous branch such as administrative services (55) we do not expect such a unique factor to exist at all.

Performing the factor analysis on the 1965 technology matrices of the five member countries of the Community individually results in considerable support for our classification. The number of admitted factors, that is, the number of eigenvalues greater than 1, as well as the index of factorization is rather stable. More important is the fact that the vast majority of factors remains well recognized in each of the countries. The following table permits a quick glance at the results.

	Factor Analyses with Stoprule "Eigenvalues > 1".	
Country	Number of Recognizable Factors	Index of Factorization
Community	15	88
Germany	14	85
France	14	86
Italy	16	87
The Netherlands	15	80
Belgium	15	80

The 16th factor in Italy happens to be the anticipated factor Hides. We there-fore consider this factor to be already identified. The absent factor in Germany is Nonferrous, while the variable nonferrous metals (8) belongs in Germany to the factor Instruments. The absent factor in France is Building; the construction industry (43) is in France related to not less than four factors.

Considering the 41 well-to-be-classified branches in the Community, the results for the five countries are also very convincing. If only a double plus sign on a "wrong" factor is considered as a real divergence, we find one divergence in Germany (due to the absence of a recognizable factor Nonferrous); two diver-gences in France, three in Italy, one in The Netherlands and one in Belgium.

Regarding the 14 problem variables, the results for the 5 countries are less favourable. The support for the a priori classification is quite firm only for the branches 11, 17 and 52. It happens repeatedly that for the other variables load-ings over .7 occur on different factors. This shows that the way in which such a branch is to be classified in the scheme for the Community, is more or less arbi-trary. For some of these branches no doubt the reason may be found in their mixed input structure; for some other branches national differences in grouping firms into branches might provide the background.

So far the analysis has yielded a classification that might be improved in two ways. First, by adding two additional factors because of the low communalities of the variables hides (34) and timber (38); second, by using another criterion for classifying the problem variables based on their loadings per country. The first operation requires a new factor analysis organised in such a fashion that it must yield 17 factors in order to give the concealed factors the opportunity to manifest themselves. This is done by replacing the stoprule mentioned by the requirement that the number of factors to be extracted has to be 17. The whole factor matrix changes, which might result in higher loadings for some of the other problem variables as well, thus solving two problems simultaneously. As a criterion by which the remaining problem variables are to be classified, we shall use the highest mean value of the loadings for the five countries instead of the largest loading for the Community.

The results of this second-stage factor analysis are shown in Table 4.1.3. Now there are 46 double plus variables to identify each of the 17 factors. Besides the fact that the variables hides (34) and timber (38) actually belong to unique fac-tors, also the brick industry (9), cement industry (10) and electrical equipment (17) are well settled. Because of two permutations in the order of their contribu-tion to the index of factorization, we list all factors again on the top of p. 75.

It is interesting to note that the sums of squares of the factor loadings on the factors Timber and Hides, respectively, are both a little over 1, thus giving sup-port once more to the extraction of the two additional factors.

1. Foods
2. Instruments
3. Chemistry and Medicines
4. Metals
5. Petro
6. Building
7. Textiles
8. Administration
9. Paper

10. Mining
11. Leather Goods
12. Automobiles
13. Nonferrous
14. Money Affairs
15. Catering
16. Timber
17. Hides

In the five countries not all 17 factors can be recognized all the time. In Germany the factor Nonferrous, which was absent originally, now does appear and so does the new factor Timber. But instead of Hides a 17th factor appears, which might have a meaning because all significant factor loadings on it are positive, but which lacks double plusses. Certainly this factor is not the factor Hides. In France the factors Building and Timber, which were absent originally, now appear. Moreover, a unique factor for variable 28 (cacao) comes in as the 17th one instead of Hides. In Italy, The Netherlands and Belgium there is no improvement in comparison with the first-stage analysis. On the contrary, the new factors lack any meaning because of alternating significant signs of their loadings. The preceding remarks imply that the index of factorization of the recognizable factors rises in the Community, Germany and France, while it falls in the other countries, as shown in the following table.

Factor Analyses with 17 Factors Extracted.		
Country	*Number of* *Recognizable Factors*	*Index of* *Factorization*
Community	17	91
Germany	16	87
France	16	89
Italy	16	86
The Netherlands	15	79
Belgium	15	79

Among the 46 double plus variables for the Community, we now find a total of 13 real divergences, of which 6 are due to the variables 9, 10, 17, 34, 38 and the remaining 7 to other variables. It is not surprising that one-half of these divergences occur at the former problem variables.

Table 4.1.3.   Classification after a Factor Analysis with 17 Extracted Factors.

Branch/Variable	Sector/Factor																
	1	2	3	4	5	6	7	8	9	10	11	12	13	14	15	16	17
1	++																
22	++																
23	++																
24	++																
25	++																
26	++																
27	++																
28	++																
29	++																
30	++																
31	++																
32	++																
6		+	+	+											+		
15		++								+							
16		++															
17		++															
21		++															
44		+											+				
48		+					+						+	+			
11			+		+	+											
12			++														
41			++														
42			+		+												
53			++					+					+				

76

13	14	19	20	2	4	45	49	9	10	43	33	37	51	52	54	55	39	40	3	5	35	36	18	47	8	50	46	38	34
																													‡
				+						+																		‡	
																											‡		
					+											+										‡			
+																									‡				
																							‡	‡					
																					‡	‡							
																			‡	‡									
					+												‡	‡											
													‡	+	‡	+													
				+							‡	‡																	
+								‡	‡	‡																			
				+	‡	+	‡	+					+			+				+									
‡	‡	‡	‡																				+						
								+					+																
		+	+							+					+														
																												+	

FA-Classification

Name	Branch Number
Foods	22–32 1
Instruments	6 15–17; 21 44 48
Chemistry and Medicines	11 12 41–42 53
Metals	7 13–14 19–20
Petro	2 4 45 49
Building	9–10 43
Textiles	33;37
Administration	51–52 54–55
Paper	39–40
Mining	3;5
Leather Goods	35–36
Automobiles	18 47
Nonferrous	8
Money Affairs	50
Catering	46
Timber	38
Hides	34

SO-Classification

Branch Number	Name
22–32	Foods
1 2	Agriculture
15–17; 21 13–14	Metals Products
11 9–10	Minerals
12	Chemical Products
6 7 8	Ores
49	Transport
4 3;5	Energy
43	Building
33;37 35;36 34	Textiles
53 51–52	Other Market Services
54–55	Administration
39–40	Paper
19–20 18	Means of Transport
44 48 45 47 46	Commerce
50	Money Affairs
41–42 38	Various Products

Figure 4.1.1. Comparison between the FA- and SO-classification of branches.

The nine remaining problem variables will be discussed one by one. The fishing (2) branch remains classified as Petro, but in Italy it clearly belongs to Textiles. The iron and nonferrous ores (6) branch remains classified as Instruments. In Germany this branch belongs to Mining. The glass (11) branch remains classified as Chemistry and Medicines. In Germany it belongs to Building. The wholesale and retail trade (45) branch remains classified as Petro. The educational and scientific research (52) branch remains classified as Administration.

The general administrative services (55) branch belongs in France to Administration and in The Netherlands to Money Affairs. The second-stage classification has been changed from Money Affairs to Administration.

Finally, there are three branches that almost certainly will suffer from interpretative difficulties because of their residual character. The products of miscellaneous industries (42) branch belong to Chemistry and Medicines in France and to Nonferrous in Italy. It remains classified as Chemistry and Medicines. The recovery and reuse (44) branch is now classified as Instruments instead of Money Affairs, whereas the repairs (48) branch remains classified as Instruments.

Having thus constructed a classification of the 55 branches into 17 sectors by means of a factor analysis of technology matrices (FA-classification), we are able to compare this classification with that of the SOEC (SO-classification). This is done in Figure 4.1.1. The numbers refer to the list of branches in Table 4.1.1.

So far, nothing has been said about the size of the sectors measured, for instance, by the value of their total input. From a purely analytic point of view, it is of no importance whether sectors incorporate small or large branches. However, it is not unreasonable to assume that the SOEC tried to form aggregates of about similar economic importance. We therefore include in the following list the total of inputs of each sector measured in billions of European Units of Account.[6]

FA-Classification		SO-Classification	
Sector	Input Total	Sector	Input Total
1 Foods	53.1	I Agriculture	17.9
2 Instruments	23.7	II Energy	13.0
3 Chemistry and Medicines	21.6	III Ores	21.0
4 Metals	27.5	IV Minerals	4.4
5 Petro	26.1	V Chemical Products	15.1
6 Building	28.3	VI Metal Products	31.3
7 Textiles	14.8	VII Means of Transport	10.0
8 Administration	21.3	VIII Foods	35.5
9 Paper	6.9	IX Textiles	17.3

FA-Classification		Input	SO-Classification		Input
	Sector	Total		Sector	Total
10	Mining	7.1	X	Paper	6.9
11	Leather Goods	1.7	XI	Various Products	8.2
12	Automobiles	11.0	XII	Building	24.6
13	Nonferrous	3.7	XIII	Commerce	23.8
14	Money Affairs	9.2	XIV	Transport	8.5
15	Catering	9.0	XV	Money Affairs	9.2
16	Timber	5.4	XVI	Other Market Services	7.9
17	Hides	0.8	XVII	Administration	16.4

It is quite clear that the FA-sectors Leather Goods and Hides are of a very small size; together they represent less than 1 percent of the overall total input. A further aggregation of these branches therefore cannot be harmful from a practical point of view. In contrast, the FA-sector Foods might be too large, representing almost 20 percent of the overall total input. Therefore, a subdivision of this sector can be defended. This kind of reasoning partially supports the SO-classification. From our point of view, the advantage of the FA-classification is, that it groups those branches into one class that possess a similar input structure. For the purpose of our analysis, distinguishing between similar branches would be meaningless.

4.2 ANALYSIS OF VARIANCE OF TECHNOLOGY MATRICES

Section 1.3 explained the way in which the method of ANOVA can be used to test whether there are significant differences in the technology matrices of several countries and whether technology matrices show significant differences in the course of time. Before this test procedure can be executed, however, a technical complication has to be solved first. In some cases, the technical coefficients a_{Ijk} (for all $j \subset J$) are very small or even zero, but differing among the countries. This results in very small variances within countries and relatively large variances among countries, leading to extremely high F-ratios. In our opinion, these particular F-ratios have little meaning. Consider, for instance, the following table of the technical coefficients a_{Ijk} in four countries, where the receiving sector consists of the two branches j_1 and j_2.

Country	Branch j_1	Branch j_2	Sector J
1	.001	.001	.001
2	0	0	0
3	0	0	0
4	0	0	0

The variance within is exactly zero and the variance among is small, yet the F-ratio becomes infinite. In the statistical sense there exists a significant difference among the countries; in this situation, however, it is not meaningful to assert that a tangible discrepancy exists among technologies. To avoid this kind of difficulty, we only computed the F-ratio for those cases in which the variance within was over .000025 (a standard deviation of .005). The reason behind the choice of this particular limit will be discussed in due course. This limitation reduces the number of calculable F-ratios to about one-half, but enough remain to perform a meaningful test on the distribution of the F-ratios over the four chosen significance intervals.

We shall begin with a discussion of the results of the international comparison of the technology matrices of Germany, France, The Netherlands and Belgium. In the following table the observed frequencies of the F-ratios and the expected frequencies under the null hypothesis are presented, both for the SO-classification and for the FA-classification.

	SO-Classification		FA-Classification	
Degree of Significance	*Observed Frequency*	*Expected Frequency*	*Observed Frequency*	*Expected Frequency*
over .25	102	102.0	83	85.5
between .25 and .10	10	20.4	16	17.1
between .10 and .05	11	6.8	5	5.7
below .05	13	6.8	10	5.7
number of F-ratios	136	136.0	114	114.0
observed χ_0^2	13.55		3.47	
$p(\chi^2 > \chi_0^2)$ $(df = 3)$	less than .01		about .30	

Observed Frequencies of F-Ratios *and Expected Frequencies under the Null Hypothesis*

It is remarkable that for both classifications the observed frequency of F-ratios

Table 4.2.1. Significance Levels of the F-Ratios for the SO-Classification.

Delivering Sector	Receiving Sector[†]												
	I	II	III	IV	VI	VII	VIII	IX	X	XI	XIII	XVI	XVII
I	0	0	–	–	–	–	0	0	0	0	0	0	–
II	0	0	0	0	0	++	0	–	0	++	0	0	0
III	–	0	0	0	0	0	–	–	–	0	0	–	–
IV	–	–	0	0	+	–	0	–	–	–	–	–	–
V	0	+	0	0	+++	+++	0	0	0	0	0	0	0
VI	++	0	+	+	0	0	0	0	–	0	0	0	0
VII	0	–	–	–	0	0	–	–	–	–	0	–	0
VIII	0	–	–	–	–	–	0	0	–	–	0	0	–
IX	0	–	–	–	–	+++	–	0	0	0	0	0	–
X	0	–	–	+	–	–	++	0	0	0	0	0	0
XI	0	–	–	0	+++	++	–	–	–	–	–	0	–
XII	–	0	–	+++	–	++	–	–	–	–	0	0	0
XIII	0	+++	0	++	+	+	+++	++	+++	0	0	++	0
XIV	0	0	+	0	+++	+	0	–	0	0	0	0	0
XV	–	–	–	–	–	–	–	–	–	–	–	–	–
XVI	–	–	–	–	–	+	–	–	0	–	0	++	0
XVII	0	0	–	–	+++	++	+++	+++	0	+++	0	0	0

Explanation of the symbols used in this table:

+++ significance level below .05

++ significance level between .10 and .05

+ significance level between .25 and .10

0 significance level over .25

– variance within countries below .000025

[†] For receiving sectors that consist of only one branch, the calculation of the variance within countries is not possible. The corresponding columns in the table are omitted.

82

Table 4.2.2. Significance Levels of the F-Ratios for the FA-Classification.

Delivering Sector	Receiving Sector[†]											
	1	2	3	4	5	6	7	8	9	10	11	12
1	0	–	0	–	0	–	0	++	0	0	–	–
2	+++	0	0	0	0	0	0	0	0	0	–	0
3	0	++	0	0	0	0	0	0	0	0	++	+
4	0	0	+	0	0	0	–	–	–	0	0	+
5	0	+++	+	+++	0	0	0	0	+	0	+++	0
6	0	+	0	0	+	0	–	0	–	0	–	–
7	–	0	0	0	0	–	0	–	–	–	0	+
8	+++	+++	+++	+++	+++	+	–	+	0	–	–	0
9	+	–	+	–	0	0	–	0	0	–	0	–
10	+	+	0	0	+	0	0	0	0	0	–	0
11	–	–	–	–	–	–	–	–	–	–	0	–
12	–	0	–	0	0	–	–	0	–	–	–	+
13	–	0	0	0	–	0	–	–	–	–	–	0
14	–	–	–	–	–	–	–	–	–	–	–	–
15	–	–		–	+++	–	–	0	–	–	–	–
16	–	++	0	0	0	0	–	–	–	–	–	–
17	–	0	–	–	–	–	0	–	–	–	++	–

Explanation of the symbols used in this table:
+++ significance level below .05
 ++ significance level between .10 and .05
  + significance level between .25 and .10
  0 significance level over .25
  – variance within countries below .000025
[†] For receiving sectors that consist of only one branch, the calculation of the variance within countries is not possible. The corresponding columns in the table are omitted.

with a significance level over .25 is almost equal to the expected frequency. For the SO-classification the highly significant χ^2-statistic for the goodness of fit is due to the small frequency of F-ratios in the region between .25 and .10 and the large frequencies in the two regions below .10. For the FA-classification there is only a slight tendency towards high F-ratios. We therefore may conclude that the FA-classification leads to aggregates that have unweighted average technical coefficients that do not differ more among countries than is to be expected by mere chance. This permits us to consolidate these countries into one economic area. For the SO-classification this procedure seems to be inadmissible because the differences among countries are too large. Not too much importance, however, should be attached to this conclusion, since the poor results for the SO-classification must be due to the suboptimality of that classification.

Although we do have confidence in this procedure to test for differences

among the countries, it is illuminating to have a closer look at the individual
F-ratios by using Tables 4.2.1 and 4.2.2. These tables enable us to determine
whether the significant F-ratios belong to particular rows and columns of the
technology matrix, that is, to particular delivering or receiving sectors. In this
fashion we obtain a better insight into the differences among countries. Under
the null hypothesis the significant F-ratios are distributed at random over these
tables. Since the null hypothesis has been rejected for the SO-classification, here
it makes sense to try and find the causes of the differences among the countries.

The structure of the significant F-ratios clearly is more rowwise than columnwise. This suggests that differences among countries are probably due to definition errors, quite likely to be the result of imperfections in the harmonizing of
the original input-output tables for each of the countries. In Table 4.2.1 the
rows XIII and XVII, corresponding to the Commerce and Administration sectors
in the SO-classification, have a large number of F-ratios that are significant at
the 10 percent level. It is interesting to note that under the FA-classification the
Administration sector (row 8 in Table 4.2.2) also creates difficulties.

Observing the columns of Table 4.2.1, Sectors VI and VII (Metal Products
and Means of Transport) are abundantly provided with double and triple plusses.
Again one of the related sectors under the FA-classification (Instruments in column 2) is of somewhat doubtful value.

It cannot be denied that there is some arbitrariness in the choice of .000025 as
the critical value of the variance within countries. Changing this limit might alter
the conclusions, because the number of calculable F-ratios depends on this limit.
Therefore, we decided to repeat the χ^2-test for some different values of this critical value. The results of this sensitivity analysis are shown in the following table:

Results of Sensitivity Analysis		
Critical Value of	Observed χ_0^2	
the Variance Within	SO-Classification	FA-Classification
.000000	89.01	90.33
.000005	32.71	8.46
.000010	25.37	4.04
.000015	21.15	4.49
.000020	16.08	4.88
.000025	13.55	3.47
.000030	16.65	1.56

The conclusions are obvious. A critical value below .000010 causes a very rapid
increase in the χ_0^2-values, pointing in the direction of the use of intangible vari-

ances within countries of the kind described in the first part of this section. The critical value .000025 seems to be rather high, but our conclusions would have remained the same for a critical value as low as .000010, since up from this level the observed χ_o^2 does not show much variation.

Sources of Variation

The typical (rowwise) pattern of the double and triple plusses in Tables 4.2.1 and 4.2.2 points towards the observation that although there are no real technological differences among the countries, there are remarkable differences in some of the technical coefficients. Therefore, we shall try to distinguish five sources of variation in the technical coefficients of the type a_{Ijk}, that is, in the coefficients on which the ANOVA has been performed. Three of these sources of variation reflect the typical problems of constructing harmonized input-output tables for several countries. The probable sources of variation are designated as follows:

I   Random Fluctuations
II   Harmonizing Failures
III   Aggregation Inaccuracies
IV   Definition Errors
V   Technological Differences

By way of illustration, we present the following simplified scheme:

I	II	III	IV	V
a a a	*a a b*	*a a b*	*b b b*	*b b b*
a a a	*a a a*	*a a b*	*a a a*	*a a a*
a a a	*a a a*	*a a b*	*a a a*	*c c c*
a a a	*a a a*	*a a b*	*a a a*	*d d d*

Blocks I through V each represent a specific structure of the technical coefficients for the combination (I,J) with three branches j in J (the columns), four countries (the rows) and one delivering sector, I. The coefficients are assumed to be random drawings from populations with the same variance; different characters symbolize the different expectations of these populations.

Block I is the only structure in full accordance with the null hypothesis of the ANOVA. Except for random fluctuations (including errors of measurement), the variances within as well as among countries are relatively low and of the same magnitude. F-ratios will not differ significantly from the value 1, except by mere chance.

In block II only one coefficient is distinct from the others. We feel that it is more likely that such a situation is due to a harmonizing failure than to a real technological difference. The variances within and among countries are both positively influenced, increasing as the difference between a and b increases. The calculated F-ratio, however, cannot serve to distinguish this situation from case I.

In block III an aggregation inaccuracy is symbolized. The variance among countries remains at the same level, while the variance within countries becomes relatively high. The calculated F-ratio may become quite low. From a purely statistical point of view, one should test for technological differences among countries after eliminating this aggregation effect, but not from the practical point of view. It should be emphasized that if one observes a clear example of an aggregation inaccuracy, this does not mean that a "better" way of aggregation will be possible, because one has to consider the consequences of another classification scheme simultaneously for all sectors and what is gained at one place might be lost at another.

In block IV all coefficients in one country differ in the same way from those in the other countries. Although it is possible that a difference in technology manifests itself in such a way, we prefer to interpret such a situation as a definition error simply because only one country is involved. This implies that only block V is to be considered as a clear-cut example of a difference in technology. It might not be easy to disentangle Situations IV and V, because in both of them the F-ratios tend to become high due to a high variance among the countries. Summarizing, the following table shows the relative magnitudes for the variances both within and among countries.

Relative Magnitudes for Variances within and among Countries			
Source of Variation	*Variance Witin*	*Variance Among*	*F-ratio*
Random Fluctuations	normal	normal	normal
Harmonizing Failures	high	high	normal
Aggregation Inaccuracies	high	normal	low
Definition Errors	normal	high	high
Technological Differences	normal	high	high

It now becomes necessary to define the borderline between high and normal variances, but it will be obvious that the variances within and among countries are not independent of the corresponding technical coefficient. An inquiry into the interdependence between the square root of the variance and the corresponding technical coefficient revealed that both variables vary greatly in size, but they are fairly well correlated with a regression coefficient of .5. Thus it is to be

Table 4.2.3. Coefficients of Variation within Countries under the FA-Classification.

Delivering Sector	Receiving Sector[†]											
	1	2	3	4	5	6	7	8	9	10	11	12
1	0.5	–	1.1	–	1.8	–	1.5	–	1.4	–	–	–
2	0.8	0.7	0.8	0.7	0.9	0.7	1.1	1.9	0.4	0.5	0.3	0.8
3	0.9	0.8	0.6	0.8	0.8	0.5	0.9	1.1	0.3	0.8	0.2	0.5
4	1.2	0.9	1.0	0.6	1.0	1.0	–	–	0.5	1.0	1.0	0.6
5	0.7	0.7	0.5	0.3	0.6	0.4	0.4	0.9	0.2	0.5	0.2	0.9
6	–	0.9	0.8	1.2	1.6	0.7	–	1.5	0.6	0.8	–	–
7	–	3.2	1.6	–	1.9	–	0.3	–	0.8	–	0.4	0.6
8	0.9	0.7	0.5	0.6	0.6	0.5	0.3	1.1	0.9	0.2	0.3	1.0
9	0.7	0.7	0.7	0.6	1.3	1.0	0.3	1.4	0.3	0.3	0.5	0.7
10	0.9	1.0	0.6	0.9	0.7	1.0	0.9	0.9	1.0	0.5	–	1.2
11	–	–	–	–	–	–	–	–	–	–	0.8	–
12	–	–	–	3.3	1.2	–	–	–	–	–	–	0.3
13	–	1.2	1.9	1.0	–	–	–	–	–	–	–	0.9
14	–	–	–	–	0.8	–	–	–	–	–	–	–
15	–	–	–	–	1.0	–	–	–	–	–	–	–
16	–	–	1.6	1.3	–	1.4	–	–	–	–	–	–
17	–	–	–	–	–	–	1.3	–	–	–	0.2	–

Explanation of the symbols used in this table:
– technical coefficient below .005
[†]For receiving sectors that consist of only one branch, the calculation of the variance within countries is not possible. The corresponding columns in the table are omitted.

expected that for all of the large technical coefficients, variances will tend to be high. Therefore, when searching for sources of variation, we shall no longer use variances as a measure of dispersion but coefficients of variation instead. The latter are defined as the square root of the variance divided by its corresponding technical coefficient. We note that in doing so, the ratio of the coefficients of variation among and within countries equals the square root of the F-ratio for the combination of I and J under study.

Tables 4.2.3 and 4.2.4 present the coefficients of variation for those sectors in the FA-classification that consist of at least two branches. If the technical coefficient $\hat{a}_{IJ}$ was below .005, however, no calculation was performed because of the low denominator. The tables reveal that even the coefficients of variation fluctuate considerably. The lowest value observed is 0.1 and the highest 3.3. We shall denote a coefficient of variation as high if a value over 1.5 is observed. Then the two tables contain a total of 13 combinations (I,J) that have at least

Table 4.2.4.   Coefficients of Variation among Countries under the FA-Classification.

Delivering Sector	Receiving Sector[†]											
	1	2	3	4	5	6	7	8	9	10	11	12
1	0.2	–	0.7	–	1.3	–	0.6	–	0.3	–	–	–
2	1.4	0.9	0.6	0.6	0.6	0.3	0.6	0.7	0.4	0.4	0.4	0.7
3	0.7	1.3	0.2	0.9	0.7	0.4	0.3	0.9	0.2	0.5	0.5	0.9
4	0.5	0.8	1.3	0.2	0.8	0.2	–	–	0.9	0.9	0.6	1.0
5	0.6	1.3	0.6	1.0	0.3	0.3	0.2	0.5	0.3	0.3	0.5	0.5
6	–	1.3	0.9	1.4	2.1	0.7	–	0.8	0.6	0.8	–	–
7	–	2.5	0.9	–	1.0	–	0.1	–	0.7	–	0.3	0.9
8	2.1	1.6	1.1	1.2	1.1	0.9	0.8	1.3	0.6	0.3	1.3	1.2
9	1.1	1.7	0.8	0.9	0.6	0.9	0.1	0.9	0.2	1.2	0.3	0.8
10	1.2	1.2	0.6	0.7	0.9	0.6	0.3	0.5	0.6	0.3	–	1.0
11	–	–	–	–	–	–	–	–	–	–	0.6	–
12	–	–	–	3.1	0.1	–	–	–	–	–	–	0.7
13	–	1.1	1.9	0.5	–	–	–	–	–	–	–	0.9
14	–	–	–	–	0.3	–	–	–	–	–	–	–
15	–	–	–	–	2.2	–	–	–	–	–	–	–
16	–	–	1.7	0.7	–	0.5	–	–	–	–	–	–
17	–	–	–	–	–	–	0.7	–	–	–	0.5	–

Explanation of the symbols used in this table:
– technical coefficient below .005
[†]For receiving sectors that consist of only one branch, the calculation of the variance within countries is not possible. The calculation of the variance among countries for those sectors therefore is not relevant; the corresponding columns in the table are omitted.

one high coefficient of variation and thus can be classified according to the sources of variation mentioned before, except for the categories IV and V that cannot be disentangled. For each of the categories II, III and IV/V we selected the clearest example of that source of variation that we could find, because these examples are quite illustrative.

The best example of a harmonizing failure is found for the combination (I,J) with $I = 12$ and $J = 4$. The coefficient of variation among countries is 3.1 and within countries 3.3 so that the F-ratio is below 1. The delivering sector in this case is Automobiles. The receiving sector is Metals, consisting of the five branches:

> 7   blast furnace products
> 13   foundry products
> 14   other metal structures
> 19   ship building
> 20   motorcycles, bicycles

The technical coefficients a_{Ijk} are shown in the following table.

Country	Technical Coefficients a_{Ijk} for I = 12, J = 4.				
	Receiving Branch				
	7	13	14	19	20
Germany	.001	.001	.001	.000	.078
France	.001	.004	.004	.005	.002
The Netherlands	.000	.000	.002	.001	.003
Belgium	.000	.000	.001	.000	.000
Average	.001	.001	.002	.002	.021

The coefficient for branch 20 in Germany is conspicious. One explanation might be that there exists a certain input in the production process of motorcycles that in Germany is observed as output from the Automobiles sector, whereas in the other countries it appears as output from another sector.

As an example of an aggregation inaccuracy the combination (I,J) with $I = 2$ and $J - 8$ is chosen. The coefficient of variation among countries is only 0.7 and within countries 1.9; thus, the F-ratio is very low. The delivering sector is Instruments, and the receiving sector is Administration, consisting of the five branches:

51 leasing of movables and real estate
52 educational and scientific research services
54 general administrative services of public administration
55 administrative services otherwise
56 domestic services

The technical coefficients a_{Ijk} are shown in the following table.

Country	Technical Coefficients a_{Ijk} for I = 2, J = 8.				
	Receiving Branch				
	51	52	54	55	56
Germany	.004	.006	.150	.016	.000
France	.002	.017	.147	.005	.000
The Netherlands	.000	.024	.075	-.008	.000
Belgium	.000	.009	.098	.000	.000
Average	.001	.014	.118	.003	.000

It is evident that branch 54 is the major user of the output of the sector Instruments. The input structure of branch 54 differs enormously from those of the four other branches regarding the input of Instruments. As stated previously, this does not imply that it would be better to classify branch 54 under a different heading, because there are 17 delivering sectors that should be taken into account when doing so.

As an example of a definition error the combination (I,J) with $I = 15$ and $J = 5$ is illustrative. The coefficient of variation among countries is 2.2 and within countries 1.0, so the F-ratio is almost 5. The delivering sector is Catering, and the receiving sector is Petro, consisting of the four branches:

  2 fishing
  4 crude petroleum, natural gas and refined products
45 wholesale and retail trade
49 transport services

The technical coefficients a_{Ijk} are shown in the following table.

Technical Coefficients a_{Ijk} for I = 15, J = 5.				
	Receiving Branch			
Country	2	4	45	49
Germany	.010	.004	.027	.013
France	.009	.002	.011	.003
The Netherlands	.000	.001	.004	.002
Belgium	.000	.000	.000	.002
Average	.005	.002	.010	.005

Although both Germany and France have technical coefficients that are considerably larger than those in the Low countries, it is hard to believe that these differences should be caused by different technologies. Catering, consisting solely of the branch lodging and catering services, is no doubt a useful, not to say an attractive ingredient of the production process, but it is hardly a cornerstone of the technology.

These three examples illustrate why we feel justified in assuming the observed differences in technical coefficients of the countries not to be of an essential character, so that consolidation of the countries is permitted. It is a pity that this consolidation has to be performed on the basis of the SO-classification, but we have seen it is reasonable to assume that this will not distort the results too much.

4.3 THE POLLUTION AND ABATEMENT COEFFICIENTS

The Choice of the Abatement Activities

A modern industrial society produces many different kinds of pollution and nuisance. Incorporating pollution abatement in our model, we had to restrict ourselves to those types for which data are available, not only on the amount of pollutant generated by one unit of each activity but also on the cost structure of the abatement activities. Furthermore, these data must fit in the SO-classification scheme.

We could not include in the model the abatement of those types of pollutant for which no technology exists or for which we could not determine the cost structure in the form necessary to our investigation. This meant we had to exclude the elimination of radioactive waste, of nonorganic chemical residuals and of nitrogen oxides as well as the abatement of noise and thermic pollution. It goes without saying that omitting the abatement of these pollutants will lead to underestimation of the cost of combating pollution. At the moment, we must operate within these limitations since the construction of the required coefficients is far beyond our means. One advantage of our modelling technique, however, is that it is not at all difficult to incorporate new activities and new rows into the model, once the necessary data become available.

The kinds of pollution we have taken into account are best specified by means of the names of their abatement activities. In total, 5 of these sectors are added to the 17 conventional sectors. Since there is a one-to-one correspondence between sectors and goods, 5 kinds of nuisance are also distinguished. The 5 new sectors are:

> XVIII Public Waste Water Treatment
> XIX Private Waste Water Treatment
> XX Desulphurization
> XXI Solid Waste Management
> XXII Adaptation of Cars and Trucks

The two first sectors remove destructable organic material from the industrial waste water. This purification is performed either by municipal enterprises (Sector XVIII) or by the polluting enterprises themselves (Sector XIX). The distinction between the two sectors (that abate the same kind of pollution) is made here, because the cost structures of these sectors are quite different. In certain cases, private purification is cheaper than public, partly because it is not necessary to make provisions for abating bacteriological pollution and because no transportation costs have to be made.

The Desulphurization sector controls pollution of the air by sulphur dioxide resulting from the burning of fossil fuels. The Energy sector is mainly responsible for this kind of pollution. Two technologies are known. The first one, the direct method, is the desulphurization of fuels. The second one, the indirect method, is the desulphurization of flue gas. Both methods are used, often in combination. The cost structure that we employed relates to such a combined technology.

Roughly speaking, there are four methods used to get rid of solid waste in an acceptable manner: controlled dumping, incineration in a destructor, converting into compost and, last but not least, recycling. Dumping and incineration are the methods used most often because they are the cheapest ones. Composting and recycling are (perhaps) more expensive but, on the other hand, possess advantages from an environmental point of view. The cost structure of Sector XXI is a weighted average of the costs of the four technologies. The weights are taken from the actual situation in The Netherlands, where composting has a minor and recycling has a negligible weight. In the future, one might expect that the weights are shifting in favour of the recycling technology and that most likely the costs of the solid waste management will rise.

Sector XXII, the adaptation of cars and trucks, is the last abatement sector. The nuisance abated by this activity is the pollution of the air with exhaust fumes from automobiles. The pollution consists of hydrocarbons, carbon monoxide, nitrogen oxides and lead compounds. The abatement technology incorporated in the model is not the purification of exhaust fumes by means of some postcombustion system, but is based on the principle of *stratified charge.* The aim of this modification of the ordinary petrol engine is to prevent or at least to reduce pollution of the air by using a CVCC engine.[7] This seems to be a satisfactory solution to this pollution problem, while its cost structure is approximately known.

The numerical data on pollution and its abatement are taken from a publication of the Central Planning Bureau of The Netherlands.[8] In this study careful estimates of pollution and abatement coefficients in The Netherlands for the year 1973 are constructed, based on available statistical information and on fact-finding. Our estimates of these coefficients for the Region are mainly based on the results obtained in this study. One point needs some discussion in advance. When using a Leontief technology, it is implicitly assumed that abatement costs per unit of pollution abated are constant. This suggests that it should be possible to obtain every desired level of purification at the same cost per unit. However, this is very unlikely. Increasing costs are inevitable, certainly in the final stages of the cost function. For our purposes this is not too troublesome, because in the model the restrictions relating to abatement are formulated in terms of "the yearly relative decrease in unabated pollution". Complete abatement is never sought, even if it could be achieved technically. Assuming an annual decrease of 10 percent, 35 percent of the original amount of unabated pollution still remains after a 10-year period, so that within the scope of this work the final parts of the cost structure are not relevant. Furthermore, one may assume that technical progress will tend to counteract the tendency toward increasing costs.

The Pollution Coefficients

The pollution coefficients for a sector are expressed as the abatement costs per unit of the production value of that sector. For the detailed data, represented by the submatrix A_{12} (see Section 1.4), the reader is referred to the appendix at the end of Chapter 4. Here, we should like to confine ourselves to a general review of these figures and to some comments. For the total economy of the Region, abatement costs as a whole do not seem to be very oppressive. They are less than 1 percent of the value of actual production. However, compared to net national income, they are more than 1.5 percent and they become nearly 3 percent and 5 percent if related to the sum of wages and the sum of other incomes, respectively. These are rather substantional portions. It should be pointed out that the picture becomes considerably darker if one looks at individual enterprises instead of at broad aggregates. Therefore, the problem of financing a pollution abatement program is certainly not a negligible one. Many excellent books have been written, all of which advocate different policies. These questions are beyond the scope of this text, since here we only try to investigate whether a given program is within the bounds imposed by the production capacity of the system. Cost elements corresponding to the abatement policies were never so excessive that sectoral profits became negative, so the incorporation of financial aspects is unnecessary.

Returning to the numerical values of the pollution coefficients, we see that Public Waste Water Treatment accounts for half the abatement costs; Adaptation of Cars and Trucks take a quarter and the three other sectors together share the last quarter. The total sectoral abatement costs range from 0 in the sector Money Affairs to 2.7 percent in the Paper sector, which is the sector that pollutes most. In the following table we have summarized the pollution data into six (groups of) sectors, representing the major economic activities, to give an impression of the total abatement costs per group and the relative importance of each of the several kinds of pollution.

Relative Distribution of Abatement Costs and Total Abatement Costs per Unit
of Production Value, for Main Sectors in the Region.

Abating Sector	Agriculture I	Energy II	Industry III/XI	Building XII	Services XIII/XVI	Government XVII	Total Economy
XVIII	–	12	65	8	21	59	50
XIX	24	3	13	–	–	–	9
XX	40	69	3	2	2	1	9
XXI	12	10	8	47	5	2	9
XXII	24	6	11	43	71	38	23
Total	100	100	100	100	100	100	100
Cost per unit	.0033	.0072	.0101	.0049	.0042	.0064	.0074

By total abatement costs per unit of the value of production, we mean the cost required to eliminate all the pollutants generated by this unit of production. Industry, with total costs of about 1 percent, is the greatest polluter per unit. As can be verified in the appendix, the costs of the industrial sectors range from 0.27 percent in the Metal Products sector to 2.70 percent in the Paper sector. High costs are also found in the Textiles sectors (1.91%), Foods (1.62%) and Chemical Products (1.57%). In all these strongly polluting industrial sectors, the main costs are caused by public waste water treatment. It is not accidental that especially in these sectors (except Textiles) the private waste water treatment causes substantial costs too, the latter no doubt being a much cheaper substitute.

Desulphurization is the largest cost factor in the Energy sector. In the Agriculture sector desulphurization is also expensive. Solid waste management is relatively and absolutely expensive in the Building sector. The adaptation of cars and trucks imposes heavy burdens on the Building sector as well as on all services sectors.

Finally, we mention the pollution coefficients for the abatement sectors themselves (the submatrix A_{22} of Section 1.4). Very important are the effluent costs for the Solid Waste Management sector and the solid waste costs for the Private Waste Water Treatment sector. Again, we refer to the appendix at the end of Chapter 4 for the complete set of data.

Cost Structure of the Abatement Activities

In the input-output matrix for the Region, the elements of the submatrix A_{12} have not yet been evaluated. The columns of this matrix reflect the cost structure of the corresponding activities. In other words, the elements of a column

Table 4.3.1. Total Investments and Annual Cost per Unit† of Each Abatement Activity‡ in Dutch Florins at 1973 Prices.

Origin	Public Waste Water Treatment		Private Waste Water Treatment		Desulphurization		Solid Waste Management		Adaptation of Cars and Trucks	
	Inv.	Costs	Inv.	Costs	Inv.	Costs	Inv.	Costs	Inv.	Costs
Industry	43	6.1	22	0.3	29	4.5	53	2.4	18	92
Building	323	1.6	13	0.2	5	0.4	19	0.1	–	–
Services	43	0.5	6	0.3	6	1.1	7	0.9	66	–
Import	22	–	23	–	36	4.9	25	0.5	198	–
Wages	–	4.5	–	0.6	–	3.6	–	5.0	–	74
Depreciation	–	16.9	–	4.3	–	5.3	–	5.5	–	–
Rents and other income	–	39.4	–	3.3	–	5.3	–	5.6	84	7
Total	431	69.0	64	9.0	76	25.1	105	20.0	366	173
Capital coefficient§	6.2		7.1		3.0		5.2		2.1	
Depreciation coefficient§	0.25		0.48		0.21		0.28		0.43	

†Public waste water treatment: data per population equivalent
 Private waste water treatment: data per population equivalent
 Desulphurization: data per ton of oil; combined fuel and flue gas desulphurization
 Solid waste management: per ton solid waste
 Adaptation of cars: by changing from a gas engine to a CVCC engine
‡Data are taken from: Central Planning Bureau of the Netherlands, Monograph no. 20
§Coefficients relative to the value of actual production

represent the inputs required per unit of each activity, that is, per unit value of actual production. Since the abatement sectors are assumed to run on a non-profit basis, the value of actual production equals the sum of intermediate inputs, wages, depreciation and rents. The basic data from which the cost structures are derived, are summarized in Table 4.3.1. For every abatement activity the annual costs and the necessary amount of capital per unit of yearly abated pollution are classified according to the origin of the inputs. From this table different sets of the model parameters can be obtained. The relative distribution of the annual costs describes the technology of the relevant activity. These figures underlie the submatrix A_{12}. From the ratio of total investments to annual costs, the capital coefficient relative to actual production can be derived; also, the corresponding depreciation coefficient can be calculated directly. These figures belong to the matrices K and D. The further evaluation of these matrices is discussed in the next section.

A short glance at Table 4.3.1 reveals the striking difference in cost structure between public and private waste water treatment. The total investments of the public sector are inflated by the high expenses for installations, systems of pipes

Table 4.3.2. Technical Coefficients for the Abatement Sectors (Submatrix A_{12})

Delivering	Abatement Sectors				
Sectors	XVIII	XIX	XX	XXI	XXII
I	–	–	–	–	–
II	.0790	.2000	.1410	.0430	.4000
III	–	–	–	–	–
IV	.0010	.0140	.0020	.0090	–
V	–	–	.2250	.0140	–
VI	.0040	.0400	.0100	.0350	–
VII	–	–	–	.0160	.1320
VIII	–	-.2400	–	–	–
IX	–	–	–	–	–
X	–	–	–	–	–
XI	.0030	.0260	.0030	.0160	–
XII	.0240	.0200	.0160	.0040	–
XIII	.0040	.0400	.0130	.0040	–
XIV	–	–	–	.0190	–
XV	.0010	–	.0010	.0040	–
XVI	.0010	–	.0020	.0100	–
XVII	.0020	–	.0040	.0170	–
Total	.1190	.1000	.4170	.1910	.5320

and the necessary improvement and expansion of the municipal sewerages, which are often not present in private systems. Otherwise, the data in this table barely need any further elucidation. We reemphasize that they are partly based on guess-work and fact-finding; thus, the data are certainly susceptible to improvement.

Regarding the construction of the submatrix A_{12}, the intermediate inputs in each of the cost vectors presented in Table 4.3.1, have to be specified according to the SO-classification in 17 conventional sectors. This has been done in Table 4.3.2. It turns out that energy is a relatively important input in the abatement activities. Except for Solid Waste Management, the technical coefficients on the use of energy are higher than those of the energy gorging conventional sectors such as Ores, Minerals, Chemical Products and Transport. Finally, a remark-able phenomenon is that the delivery of Sector VIII (Foods) to Sector XIX (Private Waste Water Treatment) is negative. The corresponding technical coeffi-cient, which is of considerable magnitude, bears a minus sign. This is due to the fact that private waste water treatment provides a by-product that can be used as cattle fodder. The minus sign of the technical coefficient indicates that this by-product is returned to the (conventional) system of production.

4.4 THE CALCULATION OF THE CAPITAL AND DEPRECIATION COEFFICIENTS

As explained in Section 1.5, the numerical values of the elements of the matrices **K** and **D** are calculated according to the formulae (1.5.7) and (1.5.8), using four types of data:

1. The relative distribution of gross investments per sector over the various kinds of investment goods: the parameters ω_{ij}.
2. The lifetime of each type of investment good: the parameters θ_j.
3. The rate of growth of real production in every sector: the parameters α_j.
4. The sectoral investment quotas: the parameters λ_j.

A brief description and justification of the way these data were gathered is now given.

The Distribution of Gross Investments

In the detailed 1965 input-output tables for the individual countries of the Region, the deliveries to the capital stock (i.e., gross capital formation) are included as a separate column of final demand, but a cross-reference table where

Table 4.4.1. Relative Distribution per Sector of Gross Investments in 1965. Germany and France Combined; Ex-works/Ex-customs Prices.

Delivering Sectors	Absorbing Sectors																	Total
	I	II	III	IV	V	VI	VII	VIII	IX	X	XI	XII	XIII	XIV	XV	XVI	XVII	
I	—	—	—	—	—	—	—	—	—	—	—	—	—	—	—	—	—	—
II	—	—	—	—	—	—	—	—	—	—	—	—	—	—	—	—	—	—
III	—	—	2	—	—	—	—	3	—	—	1	2	1	—	—	1	2	2
IV	—	—	10	—	2	2	1	13	6	5	3	10	6	4	2	2	2	2
V	5	2	4	5	36	8	5	7	—	—	6	—	—	—	2	1	1	5
VI	565	416	668	680	603	556	606	477	591	640	584	563	343	302	167	133	66	302
VII	85'	9	23	38	13	57	69	113	61	68	74	177	225	244''	50	20	8	59'''
VIII	—	—	—	—	—	—	—	—	—	—	—	—	—	—	—	—	—	—
IX	—	—	4	—	1	1	—	5	—	—	1	1	—	1	1	1	1	1
X	—	—	1	—	—	—	—	1	—	—	—	—	—	—	—	—	—	—
XI	3	2	36	3	21	10	5	47	4	2	12	9	5	2	6	8	8	9
XII	265	527	174	201	233	290	231	248	264	205	239	140	324	385	743	814	903	575
XIII	72	41	74	69	76	70	78	81	70	75	75	92	90	59	29	19	11	43
XIV	3	2	3	2	2	3	3	3	2	3	3	3	4	2	1	1	—	2
XV	—	—	—	—	—	—	—	—	—	—	—	—	—	—	—	—	—	—
XVI	—	—	—	—	—	—	—	—	—	—	—	—	—	—	—	—	—	—
XVII	2	1	1	2	13	3	2	2	2	2	2	3	2	1	—	—	—	2
Total	1000	1000	1000	1000	1000	1000	1000	1000	1000	1000	1000	1000	1000	1000	1000	1000	1000	1000

'including ships 5   ''ships 119   '''ships 7

investments are classified according to the receiving sector is absent. SOEC supplied us with these tables for Germany and for France (corresponding tables for the Benelux countries were not available). These tables were organised into 22 conventional sectors. Therefore, they had to be converted into the 17-sector SO-classification. Investments were evaluated at acquisition prices and could be compared with gross capital formation in the input-output tables. Because the variables last mentioned were evaluated at ex-works/ex-customs prices, the trade and transport margins could be calculated by subtraction. These margins, which primarily occur at the purchase of machinery and equipment and of cars, are deliveries from Sectors XIII (Commerce) and XIV (Transport). We have distributed these margins over the investing sectors in proportion to the relevant investments. Next, the German and French tables were added and transformed into fractions of the column totals. The result is presented in Table 4.4.1.

Apart from all details, the table reflects the well-known fact that the investment good "machinery and equipment" (delivered by Sector VI) is relatively more important in the industrial sectors (III up to and including XI) and that the investment good "building" (delivered by Sector XII) is of great importance in the Energy sector (II), the services sectors (XIII up to and including XVI) and completely dominates in the Administration sector (XVII).

The Lifetime of Each Type of Investment Good

According to the current definition of an investment good in input-output studies, its lifetime has to be more than 1 year. If not, it is said to be an intermediate good. Referring to Table 4.4.1 and ignoring those delivering sectors that contribute less than a half percent to total gross investments, only 6 out of 17 sectors produce and distribute investment goods. Henceforth we shall confine ourselves to these 6 sectors. The investment goods they produce are to be called:

chemical equipment: Delivered by Sector V
machinery and equipment: Delivered by Sector VI
cars and trucks; ships: Delivered by Sector VII
wooden products: Delivered by Sector XI
buildings: Delivered by Sector XII
margins: Delivered by Sector XIII

We possess no observational data on the "mean" lifetime of the wide range of goods within each category. To make progress we made estimates on the basis of common sense; the results are shown in Table 4.4.2.

Table 4.4.2. The Lifetime in Years of Investment Goods within Each Sector.

Type of Investment Good	Investing Sector							
	I	II	III	IV–XIII	XIV	XV	XVI	XVII
chemical equipment	5	5	5	5	5	5	5	5
machinery and equipment	10	15	15	10	10	10	10	10
cars and trucks	5	5	5	5	5	5	5	5
ships	15	–	–	–	15	–	–	–
wooden products	5	5	5	5	5	5	5	5
buildings	40	40	30	30	30	30	40	50
margins	9	14	14	9	9	9	9	9

For machinery and equipment a lifetime of 10 years is assumed for most sectors; it is set at 15 years for the Energy and Ores sectors only. More variation in lifetime is assumed for the most important investment good, buildings. It is set at 30 years for the industrial and commercial sectors, at 40 years for the Agriculture, Energy and Other Market Services sectors and at 50 years in the Administration sector. The lifetime of margins is supposed to be a weighted average of the lifetimes of all capital goods, buildings and ships excluded.

The Rate of Growth of Real Production

Much is known about the rate of growth of real production; in particular, about the development of national income in constant prices. Its series are published in most countries nowadays. We own to Kuznets[9] a broad collection of historical data on this item for many countries. From the beginning of the century until 1965, real production in the countries of Western Europe increased at the rate of 2 to 3 percent per annum. In the early sixties, however, growth was much faster. From the year 1960 on, SOEC publishes the volume indices of gross domestic product for the separate countries of the European Economic Community (EEC) (for The Netherlands from 1963 on) which show on the average a growth rate of more than 5 percent over the 6-year period 1960–1965 and less than 5 percent over the 10-year period 1965–1974. Details are presented on the next page.

The actual investments in 1965 are the result of investment decisions by entrepreneurs based on actual growth of demand in recent years and on expectations about the near future, so the observed rates of growth in the period 1960–1965 will be of more interest than older data such as those gathered by Kuznets. The Kuznets data are only mentioned here to show that the period 1960–1965

Rates of Growth of Total Product, in Constant Prices.			
		SOEC	
	Kuznets	*1960–1965*	*1965–1974*
Germany (F.R.)	1936–1967: 3.9%	4.8%	4.3%
France	1896–1966: 2.1%	5.8%	5.3%
The Netherlands	1900–1967: 2.8%	–	5.2%
Belgium	1900–1967: 1.9%	5.0%	5.0%

is obviously characterized by an accelerated growth, which implies that during that period generally no parts of the capital stock will be idle. Because of this, we can employ the vintage model of Section 1.5 in which the degree of utilisation of the capital stock is not included.

Regarding real growth in the various sectors, much variation around the mean rate of 5 percent can be expected. Indeed, we found rates varying from 1 percent in the Agriculture sector to 10 percent in the Chemical Products sector. SOEC has published several kinds of data on the development of real production per sector for the separate countries of the Community, in the form of time series. The harmonization of the national accounts, however, had not yet made much progress in the early sixties. For some members of the Community the subdivision into sectors and branches was more detailed than for others. Also, the definition of production was not always uniform. For our purpose, the series entitled "gross national product at market prices per branch", in constant prices of 1963 (for Germany 1962) seemed to be best. For all countries, except for The Netherlands, these time series were available. From these series the actual rates of growth of real production were estimated for Germany and France combined and these rates were related to the investment data for these countries, as explained earlier. The results are presented in column (2) of Table 4.4.3.

In the same table the growth rates per sector of labour productivity (β_j) and of the labour force (γ_j) are shown. Although these data are not directly involved in the calculation of k_j and d_j, we will pay some attention to them because they as well as α_j illustrate the actual development of the economic system up to the year 1965, the starting point of our dynamic model. Data on the labour force are taken from SOEC publications too; the growth rates of labour productivity are computed with the aid of these data. Unfortunately, the data on the development of the labour force in the industry were published only for the manufacturing industry as a whole (Sectors III up to and including XI combined). It is assumed that the calculated labour productivity of this aggregate is also valid for its component sectors. The growth rates of the labour force in these sectors can now be estimated. Column (3) of Table 4.4.3 contains the results of the calculations. The sectors for which growth rates of labour productivity could be cal-

Table 4.4.3. Some Data on Growth and Investments per Sector in 1965; Germany and France combined.

(1)	α_j (2)	β_j (3)	γ_j (4)	z_j (5)	g_j (6)	λ_j^* (7)	d_j^* (8)	k_j^* (9)
I Agriculture	.011	.051	-.038	12,961	2,795	.2156	.180	3.24
II Energy	.039	.065	-.027	11,321	3,588	.3169	.122	5.00
III Ores	.028	.052	-.023	4,317	1,286	.2479	.191	3.83
IV Minerals	.068	.052	.015	4,495	1,067	.2374	.108	1.91
V Chemical Products	.099	.052	.045	7,163	2,556	.3568	.119	2.41
VI Metal Products	.073	.052	.020	23,643	2,334	.0987	.040	0.80
VII Means of Transport	.063	.052	.010	4,693	1,178	.2510	.119	2.10
VIII Foods	.049	.052	-.003	11,788	1,454	.1233	.069	1.11
IX Textiles	.038	.052	-.013	7,903	739	.0935	.057	0.97
X Paper	.051	.052	-.001	4,608	614	.1332	.073	1.19
XI Various Products	.063	.052	.010	5,145	772	.1500	.071	1.26
XII Building	.071	.036	.034	19,448	1,859	.0956	.047	0.68
XIII Commerce	.052	.040	.012	34,940	3,422	.0979	.051	0.90
XIV Transport	.047	.039	.008	11,149	3,142	.2818	.139	3.04
XV Money Affairs	.062	.012	.051	1,488	594	.3992	.110	4.67
XVI Other Market Services	.053	.038	.015	19,987	19,107	.9559	.211	14.06
XVII Administration	.033	.014	.019	24,060	8,316	.3456	.087	7.85
Total	.053	.046	.006	209,109	54,825	.2622	.096	3.62

α = growth rate of real production

β = growth rate of labour productivity

γ = growth rate of labour force

z = gross value added at market prices in millions of EUR

g = total investments in millions of EUR

λ^* = sectoral investment quota relative to z

d^* = depreciation coefficient relative to z

k^* = capital coefficient relative to z

culated do not show great variation in this respect, with the exception of the administrative sectors such as Money Affairs and Administration. These show a very small growth rate, which illustrates that the computer age had not made its entry into Europe in the early sixties.

The rates of growth of the labour force, presented in column (4), show much more variation. Worth mentioning are the pronounced depopulation of the Agriculture sector at a rate of almost 4 percent annually, which is due to the transition to larger scale production; the declining labour force in the Energy sector (the closing down of coal mines) and in the Ores and Textiles sectors, which is due to low-cost foreign competition. On the other hand, pronounced increases in the labour force are observed in the Chemical Products, Building and Money Affairs sectors. These figures illustrate the change that has passed over the Western European production process during the early sixties.

In our opinion the estimated growth rates of labour productivity are plausible with respect to their relative differences and modest dispersion. As far as data on the development of the labour force are available, the growth rate of labour productivity can thus serve as a check on the estimated growth rate of real production for a sector. For the sectors within the manufacturing industry, this check is not applicable. Accepting the growth rate in labour productivity in the industrial sectors as a datum, the estimated growth rate of real production can be tested by means of the resulting figures for the development of the labour force.

The Sectoral Investment Quotas

To apply Formulae (1.5.7) and (1.5.8), the sectoral investment quotas λ_j are the remaining parameters to be estimated. This was done by first calculating the investment quotas with respect to gross value added:

$$\lambda_j^* = \frac{g_j}{z_j}$$

This leads to estimates of the capital and depreciation coefficients to be denoted by k_j^* and d_j^*, respectively, which are also relative to gross value added. Since these coefficients are more familiar to economists than the k_j and d_j, intuition can serve better by examining the plausibility of the results of the computations. The λ_j^*'s are calculated for Germany and France combined. Once more we assume them to be valid for The Netherlands and Belgium as well. The resulting sectoral capital and depreciation coefficients are presented in columns (8) and (9) of Table 4.4.3. A short glance at the last three columns of this table reveals that in spite of (or perhaps thanks to) all necessary assumptions and guesses, the results of the calculations are quite plausible. For the "total economy" we find a capital coefficient of 3.6 and a depreciation rate of .10. Both values are reasonable and agree with the observed investment quota of .28 for the total economy. That is, λ^* is about equal to $\alpha k^* + d^*$, or: $.28 = .05 \times 3.6 + .10$.

Within the industrial sectors larger values for k_j^* are found in the heavy industries (Energy, Ores and Chemical Products) than in the other sectors. Notable and unexpected are the small values for k and d in the very important Metal Products sector. Algebraically this is the result of a relatively small sectoral investment quota, due to a relatively high labour quota in this sector. In Sector XVI (Other Market Services) which contains, among others, the branches health services and leasing of real estate, a very large capital coefficient is noticeable. The value found is plausible where the leasing of real estate is concerned, but for the health services it is not. Here we are confronted with one of the main objections that can be put forward against the SOEC classification of branches into a relatively small number of sectors, where the classification criterion is not attuned to the specific wishes of the user of the statistical data. For our purpose, an optimal way of aggregation is one for which branches with a similar input structure are to be joined into one sector. The input structure of the health services resembles that of the Chemical Products sector much more than that of the leasing of real estate. For the health services a capital coefficient of 2.4, as found for the chemical industry, is more reasonable than the value of 14 we found for the opaque Sector XVI. As previously stated, the absence of detailed data on investment forced us to calculate the matrices **K** and **D** in the SO-classification, although a better classification was constructed in Section 4.1.

The Matrices **K** and **D** in the Leontief Equations

On behalf of the Leontief equations, all coefficients in the matrices **K** and **D** must be calculated relative to the value of actual production instead of relative to gross value added. This leads to (much) lower values than are reported in Table 4.4.3, since in every sector the value of actual production equals gross value added plus all intermediate inputs (inclusive imports) absorbed by that sector. If intermediate inputs are relatively high compared to the value of actual production, as in the case of the Ores (79%), Foods (70%) and Money Affairs (80%) sectors, the coefficients decrease considerably. When the opposite is true, as in the case of the Commerce (30%), Transport (33%), Other Market Services (20%) and Administration (30%) sectors, the decrease is small. By using for each sector the proportion of gross value added to actual production, the matrices **K** and **D** relative to gross value added are converted to those we need. The latter ones, specified completely in the appendix at the end of this chapter, will be used in the model computations.

APPENDIX TABLES

Appendix 4A. List of (Abbreviated) Names of the 22 Sectors of the Full Model

Code	(Abbreviated) Names
I	Agriculture
II	Energy
III	Ores
IV	Minerals
V	Chemical Products
VI	Metal Products
VII	Means of Transport
VIII	Foods
IX	Textiles
X	Paper
XI	Various Products
XII	Building
XIII	Commerce
XIV	Transport
XV	Money Affairs
XVI	Other Market Services
XVII	Administration
XVIII	Public Waste Water Treatment
XIX	Private Waste Water Treatment
XX	Desulphurization
XXI	Solid Waste Management
XXII	Adaptation of Cars and Trucks

Appendix 4B.   Matrix **A** of Technical Coefficients for the Region in 1965 ($\times$ 10^{-4}).

Sectors	I	II	III	IV	V	VI	VII	*Conventional Sectors* VIII	IX	X	XI
I	1,632	27	1	7	83	—	1	4,346	629	180	612
II	183	3,325	791	1,009	736	207	148	174	164	314	226
III	18	58	5,516	126	160	1,282	774	8	9	42	118
IV	32	21	124	919	288	77	52	47	7	32	89
V	416	196	96	253	2,552	255	268	82	660	354	785
VI	196	293	257	289	384	2,045	1,509	173	113	176	335
VII	8	—	—	1	1	86	2,344	2	—	—	2
VIII	1,477	4	4	4	226	5	4	1,285	147	10	14
IX	39	10	6	17	66	45	163	16	3,588	100	486
X	24	56	56	193	345	102	61	173	124	2,910	129
XI	36	39	26	137	61	148	389	33	127	35	1,925
XII	75	114	34	111	72	68	54	22	39	48	54
XIII	289	151	487	412	328	300	218	296	310	392	361
XIV	142	228	317	381	278	192	159	164	167	300	260
XV	36	35	24	30	33	29	26	23	30	41	45
XVI	66	32	21	39	82	76	38	32	28	94	27
XVII	57	106	93	223	224	199	156	104	119	294	168
XVIII	—	9	5	17	111	6	33	111	150	210	17
XIX	8	2	2	—	25	—	—	39	1	45	—
XX	13	50	9	5	5	—	—	1	2	4	5
XXI	4	7	7	12	9	6	10	3	20	3	12
XXII	8	4	3	17	7	15	20	8	18	8	17
Wage Quota	693	2,015	1,267	3,148	2,107	3,114	2,423	1,023	2,361	2,792	2,503

							Abatement Sectors			
XII	XIII	XIV	XV	XVI	XVII	XVIII	XIX	XX	XXI	XXII
23	95	7	—	41	14	—	—	—	—	—
183	280	796	119	211	284	790	2,000	1,410	430	4,000
461	30	37	—	14	13	—	—	—	—	—
1,231	16	8	—	21	20	10	140	20	90	—
210	58	47	21	159	95	—	—	2,250	140	—
1,003	251	247	96	115	666	40	400	100	350	—
1	134	198	—	3	87	—	—	—	160	1,320
3	695	53	4	108	37	—	-2,400		—	—
25	63	22	5	41	38	—	—	—	—	—
70	272	77	265	95	329	—	—	—	—	—
624	56	94	6	59	49	30	260	30	160	—
24	60	225	70	527	300	240	200	160	40	—
457	453	430	171	169	261	40	400	130	40	—
273	273	698	349	88	242	—	—	—	190	—
33	70	88	5,227	45	49	10	—	10	40	—
24	83	106	121	64	159	10		20	100	—
426	143	126	1,529	275	357	20	—	40	170	—
4	5	1	—	23	38	—	—	—	2,022	—
—	—	—	—	—	—	—	—	—	—	—
1	1	—	—	—	1	—	—	—	—	—
23	2	1	—	1	1	260	1,281	—	—	—
21	40	37	1	15	24	4	19	2	42	—
2,968	2,577	4,339	3,848	3,652	5,026	650	670	1,430	2,500	—

Appendix 4C.1. Matrix **D** of Depreciation Coefficients for the Region in 1965 ($\times$ 10^{-4}).

Sectors	*Conventional Sectors*										
	I	*II*	*III*	*IV*	*V*	*VI*	*VII*	*VIII*	*IX*	*X*	*XI*
V	5	3	9	5	35	3	4	7	2	2	5
VI	576	395	283	488	341	134	300	109	143	242	208
VII	91	13	13	40	12	20	47	33	18	33	35
XI	3	2	22	2	20	3	3	16	1	1	6
XII	195	192	49	39	20	17	34	22	30	29	25
XIII	79	43	34	56	57	19	44	22	18	32	30
Σ	949	648	410	630	485	196	432	209	212	339	309

Appendix 4C.2. Matrix **K** of Capital Coefficients for the Region in 1965.

Sectors	*Conventional Sectors*										
	I	*II*	*III*	*IV*	*V*	*VI*	*VII*	*VIII*	*IX*	*X*	*XI*
V	—	—	—	—	0.22	—	—	—	—	—	—
VI	0.61	0.78	0.52	0.68	0.55	0.19	0.40	0.14	0.17	0.31	0.28
VII	0.05	0.01	0.01	0.02	0.01	0.01	0.03	0.02	0.01	0.02	0.02
XI	—	—	0.01	—	0.01	—	—	0.01	—	—	—
XII	0.98	0.78	0.02	0.36	0.32	0.17	0.28	0.15	0.16	0.19	0.21
XIII	0.07	0.08	0.06	0.06	0.07	0.02	0.05	0.02	0.02	0.04	0.04
Σ	1.71	2.65	0.82	1.12	0.98	0.39	0.76	0.34	0.36	0.56	0.55

	Conventional Sectors						Abatement Sectors				
XII	XIII	XIV	XV	XVI	XVII		XVIII	XIX	XX	XXI	XXII
3	3	6	1	23	6		–	–	–	–	–
136	142	364	72	604	116		610	3,800	1,880	1,970	100
59	119	302	30	118	17		40	–	–	2,000	4,180
3	3	3	4	53	17		–	–	–	–	–
8	48	185	98	785	432		1,350	470	60	320	–
25	41	78	15	96	20		450	510	170	260	–
234	356	938	222	1,679	608		2,450	4,780	2,110	2,750	4,280

	Conventional Sectors						Abatement Sectors				
XII	XIII	XIV	XV	XVI	XVII		XVIII	XIX	XX	XXI	XXII
–	–	–	–	0.01	0.01		–	–	–	–	–
0.19	0.18	0.45	0.10	0.77	0.13		0.92	5.02	2.60	3.83	0.10
0.03	0.07	0.35	0.02	0.07	0.01		0.02	–	–	0.10	1.64
–	–	–	–	0.03	0.01		–	–	–	–	–
0.08	0.34	1.17	0.80	10.21	5.31		4.68	1.41	0.18	0.95	–
0.03	0.04	0.08	0.02	0.10	0.02		0.63	0.68	0.24	0.37	.38
0.33	0.63	2.05	0.94	11.19	5.49		6.25	7.11	3.02	5.25	2.12

Appendix 4D. Initial Data for the Region in 1965 (in Million EUR).†

Sectors	Production Capacity	Actual Production	Intermed. Deliveries	Consumption	Depreciation	Net Investments	Export Surplus
I	7,050	7,030	8,008	2,130	—	—	-3,108
II	10,170	10,140	8,022	2,180	—	—	- 62
III	12,960	12,920	10,262	0	—	—	2,658
IV	2,540	2,530	2,504	160	—	—	- 134
V	7,010	6,990	4,556	1,060	106	50	1,218
VI	14,900	14,860	7,925	1,600	3,645	1,780	- 90
VII	3,530	3,520	1,442	1,100	871	600	- 493
VIII	13,300	13,260	4,470	9,260	—	—	- 470
IX	8,030	8,010	3,554	4,100	—	—	356
X	3,410	3,400	3,134	610	—	—	- 344
XI	3,040	3,030	2,307	1,360	160	70	- 867
XII	12,360	12,320	1,670	240	2,034	9,020	- 644
XIII	17,850	17,800	4,900	11,540	581	250	529
XIV	6,840	6,820	3,660	1,590	—	—	1,570
XV	2,580	2,570	1,926	750	—	—	- 106
XVI	9,650	9,620	933	9,290	—	—	- 603
XVII	11,730	11,700	3,156	9,230	—	—	- 686
Total	146,950	146,520	72,429	56,200	7,397	11,770	-1,276
XVIII	—	0	—	-610	—	—	—
XIX	—	0	—	-110	—	—	—
XX	—	0	—	-100	—	—	—
XXI	—	0	—	-120	—	—	—
XXII	—	0	—	-280	—	—	—

†In 1965, the European Unit of Account was the U.S. dollar. SOEC has converted the national currencies involved, according to: 1 EUR = 4 German marks; = 4.937 French francs; = 3.62 Dutch florins; = 50 Belgian francs.

5 DIFFERENT SCENARIOS FOR THE TEST MODEL

5.1 INTRODUCTION

In this chapter we discuss the results of some computations that have been performed with the test model. Referring to Chapter 3 for details, we repeat that this test model consists of only four sectors; the first two delivering both investment goods and consumption goods, the third delivering consumption goods only, while the last one is the pollution abatement sector.

The computations have been done as well with the year-to-year optimization model as with the 10-year model. As is explained in detail in Chapter 3, two essentially different investment models have been used to fix the expansion of productive capacity in the system under year-to-year optimization. These two models can be characterized briefly as follows:

1. In investment model I, the investment decisions are based on the shadow prices of the sectoral production capacities. These prices measure the scarcity of the capital goods. In this investment model, the expansion of the capacity is generated by the solution of an LP-problem in which all variable coefficients are supplied by a solution of the production model. Because a shadow price of the production model measures the increase of

the wage sum if capacity were increased by one unit, the maximization of the objective function of the investment model distributes investments such that the *increase* of the wage sum is maximized.

2. In investment model II, the expansion of the capacity in each sector is made proportional to the product of the existing capacity in that sector and the corresponding shadow price. The expansion of large sectors tends to be larger than that of small sectors in absolute terms. Investment model II is not formulated as an LP-problem; the goods available for investment are allocated in a direct manner to the sectors for expansion of their productive capacity.

Table 5.1.1 shows the numerical values of the fixed coefficients of the test model. In the year-to-year optimization these coefficients determine the results of the production model. The 16 rows of this scheme represent for each sector a Leontief, a capacity, a disinvestment and a political restriction. The coefficients pertaining to the objective function—the wage shares in actual production—are added as a separate row. The numerical values of the initial conditions are presented at the bottom of the table. After the explanation of the model in Chapter 2, the structure of this scheme will be clear. The socioeconomic relations included in this model prevent the decrease of capacity and of conventional consumption in any sector and require nuisance to decrease at a rate of at least 10 percent annually. Regarding the initial conditions for the system, we note that it was not possible to start with zero capacity for the abatement sector, perhaps the most obvious choice. Investment model II would not work in that case because expansion in the abatement sector would remain zero, making the comparison between the two variants of the investment model impossible. We were compelled to start with a positive initial capacity for the abatement sector.[1]

As stated in Chapter 3, in the case of the year-to-year optimization procedures, several provisions had to be made to prevent the system from becoming infeasible prematurely. In the production model, measures were taken to weaken the socioeconomic restrictions we originally had in mind. To this end, the minimal rate of the decrease of nuisance was reduced from 10 percent to 5 percent annually, and the increase of conventional consumption was modified by taking into account a consumption-habituation ratio of one half. Furthermore, some minimal investments in the abatement sector were enforced in advance, to an extent corresponding with next years' decrease in allowed nuisance. Finally, but only in investment model I, the expansion of capacity was limited by means of the introduction of *range conditions,* to be explained in the next section.

After these preliminary adjustments were made, it was possible to keep the system alive for at least ten successive years. In Section 5.2 the behaviour of the system incorporating investment model I is investigated. In Section 5.3 this is

Table 5.1.1. LP-Scheme for the Test Model with 4 Sectors.

Restrictions	Production (t)				Capacity (t+1)				Capacity (t)				Consumption (t)				Consumption (t-1)				Sign	Right-hand Side
	x_1	x_2	x_3	x_4	w_1	w_2	w_3	w_4	w_1	w_2	w_3	w_4	f_1	f_2	f_3	f_4	f_1	f_2	f_3	f_4		
1	.889	-.058	-.082	-.131	-.28	-.56	-3.11	-3.11	.28	.56	3.11	3.11	-1								$\geq$	0
2 Leontief	-.197	.493	-.140	-.418	-.27	-.47	-.41	-1.90	.27	.47	.41	1.90		-1							$\geq$	0
3 Restrictions	-.144	-.066	.688	.014											-1						$\geq$	0
4	-.005	-.007	-.009	.956												-1					$=$	0
5	1								-1												$\leq$	0
6 Capacity		1								-1											$\leq$	0
7 Restrictions			1								-1										$\leq$	0
8				1								-1									$\leq$	0
9					1				-1												$\geq$	0
10 Disinvestment						1				-1											$\geq$	0
11 Restrictions							1				-1										$\geq$	0
12								1				-1									$\geq$	0
13													1				-1				$\geq$	0
14 Political														1				-1			$\geq$	0
15 Restrictions															1				-1		$\geq$	0
16																1				-.90	$\leq$	0
Wage Share	.28	.22	.29	.07																		

Initial conditions for the system:

$w_1(t=1) = 32{,}500 \qquad f_1(t=0) = 12{,}000$

$w_2(t=1) = 55{,}000 \qquad f_2(t=0) = 10{,}000$

$w_3(t=1) = 59{,}000 \qquad f_3(t=0) = 33{,}000$

$w_4(t=1) = 350 \qquad f_4(t=0) = 833.33$

done for the system with investment model II, while in Section 5.4 the results of
the 10-year optimization of the test model are discussed.

5.2   YEAR-TO-YEAR OPTIMIZATION WITH INVESTMENT MODEL I

The most interesting series produced by a 10-year run of this variant of the year-
to-year optimization model are presented in Table 5.2.1. The series included in
this table are actual production, capacity, consumption, nuisance and the annual
wage sum. The performance of this variant is not very impressive. It is true that
the system is capable of satisfying all the demands made on it, but that was
where all the preliminary adjustments were made for. It is also true that the
annual wage sum increased by 11 percent in 9 years. This growth, however, was
achieved during the first 5 years only; thereafter the value of the objective function remained constant. As a matter of fact, the whole system became stationary
after the sixth year.

In investment model I, the vector y of the capacity expansions is chosen to
maximize the scalar $p'y$, where p represents the vector of the shadow prices on
the capacity restrictions of the production model. The values of the elements of
this vector are supplied by the solution of the production model, briefly called
the *production plan*. The maximization is subject to two sets of restrictions,
namely $Ky \leqslant s$ and $y \leqslant r$. The former indicates that the capacity expansions are
bounded by the Leontief slacks. These slacks are also supplied by the production
plan, with the claims for enforced investments in the abatement sector already
deducted. The restrictions $y \leqslant r$ are the so-called range conditions; the values of
the elements of the vector r are supplied by the production plan too. They are
the range limits, indicating how far a binding capacity restriction could be
widened without changing its shadow price.

The range conditions play a very important role in this variant of the model.
Studying the output of the simulations, it becomes obvious that they protect
the investors from investing in any sector to such an extent that the next year
the newly created capacity has to remain unused, either because the nuisance
would exceed the admitted level, or because the Leontief restrictions on the conventional goods would be violated. One advantage of the small size of the test
model is that the working of the range conditions can be traced in detail. Table
5.1.1[2] can be used to verify how the solution of the investment model (presented in Table 5.2.1) for the first year is reached.

In the first year, nuisance is not allowed to exceed a value of 750. According
to Table 5.2.1 the production plan generates a nuisance of 744. All production is
at full capacity; the shadow prices on the capacity restrictions, therefore, equal
the wage shares of the corresponding activities. Under these circumstances,

investment model I would prefer to invest all the available slack in the first sector of the test model were it not for the range conditions. Because of these range conditions, the investment plan according to model I is not that one-sided. Additional production in the first sector implies additional pollution. The nuisance, however, can only be increased up to 750 — the upper limit for the first year. Production in the first sector, therefore, can only be increased to the extent that the additional pollution does not exceed 750 − 744 = 6 units. The computer solution works with the more exact amount of 6.1 units. The pollution coefficient of the first sector equals .005. Therefore, production in this sector can only be increased by 6.1/.005 = 1220 units, and this is the numerical value of the range limit for y_1.

In the same way, the range conditions on the expansions of the capacity of the other conventional sectors can be calculated. The MPSX/370 package contains a procedure called RANGE, which computes the range limits. These limits are partial ones in the sense that they are computed one by one, each limit independent from the others. We arrived at the following results because of some rounding errors:

$$r_1 = \frac{6.1}{.005} = 1210$$

$$r_2 = \frac{6.1}{.007} = 870$$

$$r_3 = \frac{6.1}{.009} = 670$$

There are enough investment goods available to enable the capacity expansion in the three sectors to be increased up to these range limits. The remaining part of the slacks from the production model is then used to invest in the abatement sector. Before the range condition in this sector could become active, the slack s_2 is completely exhausted. What is left from the slack s_1 goes to consumption. As shown in Table 5.2.1, the increase in f_1 is considerable. Because in this first year the range conditions for the conventional sectors are rather tight, the increase in the capacity of the abatement sector is so substantial that from the second year onwards, allowed nuisance plays no longer a role in determining the range limits. From that year on these are fixed by the Leontief restrictions on the conventional goods. The successive vectors y in Table 5.2.1 can be exhaustively explained by the preceding kind of reasoning.

In a sense the range conditions do cure some aspects of the myopia of the model; however, they do not protect the system against vanishing growth. Because the expansion of the capacity in the second sector does not keep up with

Table 5.2.1. Main Results for the Year-to-Year Optimization with the Test Model; Investment Model I with Range Conditions from Production Model.

Year	Production				Expansion of Capacity				Consumption/Nuisance				Wage Sum
	x_1	x_2	x_3	x_4	y_1	y_2	y_3	y_4	f_1	f_2	f_3	f_4	
1	32,500	55,000	59,000	350	1,210	870	670	682	15,788	10,000	33,262	744	38,335
2	33,710	55,870	59,670	1,032	3,562	492	2,085	6	13,894	10,000	33,537	110	39,107
3	37,272	56,362	61,728	1,038	4,716	—	—	7	23,193	10,000	34,514	145	40,810
4	41,988	56,362	61,728	1,045	462	—	490	8	27,025	10,000	33,977	161	42,130
5	42,450	56,362	62,218	1,053	547	—	—	8	28,871	10,000	34,262	160	42,403
6	42,997	56,362	62,218	1,061	80	—	—	7	29,462	10,000	34,199	155	42,556
7	43,077	56,362	62,218	1,034†	—	—	—	10	29,532	10,000	34,190	182	42,577
8	43,077	56,362	62,218	981†	—	—	—	11	29,502	10,000	34,189	232	42,573
9	43,077	56,362	62,218	913†	—	—	—	15	29,465	10,000	34,188	297	42,568
10	43,077	56,362	62,218	827†	—	—	—	19	29,417	10,000	34,187	379	42,562

Table 5.3.1. Main Results for the Year-to-Year Optimization in the Test Model; Investment Model II.

Year	Production				Expansion of Capacity				Consumption/Nuisance				Wage Sum
	x_1	x_2	x_3	x_4	y_1	y_2	y_3	y_4	f_1	f_2	f_3	f_4	
1	32,500	55,000	59,000	350	1,265	1,682	2,378	41	12,000	10,122	33,262	744	38,335
2	33,765	52,098†	61,378	391	26	—	3	109	21,556	10,061	34,945	712	38,743
3	33,791	56,682	61,381	500	694	915	1,306	34	16,778	11,267	34,644	640	39,767
4	34,485	57,597	62,687	534	760	997	1,431	35	16,778	11,276	35,403	629	40,544
5	35,245	57,318†	64,118	569	137	—	14	572	20,814	10,970	36,320	611	41,112
6	35,382	58,594	64,132	1,141	559	727	1,049	8	18,796	11,522	36,238	74	41,476
7	35,941	59,321	65,181	1,149	612	794	1,150	9	18,796	11,532	36,849	83	42,097
8	36,553	60,115	66,331	1,158	670	866	1,260	10	18,796	11,541	37,517	93	42,777
9	37,223	60,981	67,591	1,168	735	945	1,381	11	18,796	11,551	38,250	105	43,522
10	37,958	61,926	68,972	1,179	804	1,031	1,514	12	18,796	11,558	39,055	117	44,336

† production below capacity

that in the first sector, the second sector becomes unable to deliver investment goods and the system is stagnant after the sixth year.

Returning to the investment scheme for the first year, with its large increase in the capacity of the abatement sector, note that in that year the nuisance problem is solved in one stroke for many successive years. From the second year on, nuisance is (far) below its allowed level. Even from the seventh year on, actual production in the abatement sector is below capacity. This sector uses inputs from the other conventional sectors, which can be employed more profitably elsewhere. Looking at the Figure 5.1, where the time series over 10 years are drawn for actual and admitted nuisance, one gets the impression that the two preliminary adjustments of the model regarding the annual rate of decrease of nuisance and the enforcement of investments in the abatement sector could have been omitted as well.

But it is not correct to consider these adjustments to be completely superfluous. It is only because of the specific range conditions in the first year – depending on the arbitrarily chosen initial value for f_4 – that the political restriction on nuisance after the first year is never binding anymore. Moreover, the enforced investments in the abatement sector add up to a total of 109 in the ninth year, so for the tenth year this restriction is not binding only because of these enforced investments in previous years. Regarding the weakening of the annual rate of decrease of nuisance from 10 percent to 5 percent, the same argument holds. We see from Figure 5.1 that a 10 percent version would have given the same general picture as the 5 percent version (presented in Table 5.2.1) except for the tenth year.

The most important adjustment in the (production) model certainly was the introduction of the consumption-habituation ratio of one-half. As stated previously, this adjustment was intended to weaken the restrictions on conventional consumption in favour of an increase in the supply of investment goods. The political restrictions on consumption were changed in such a fashion that consumption in year t now at least has to equal a standard for that year, which might be lower than the previous year's consumption. The standard for this year (denoted by $\bar{f_t}$) equals the standard for the previous year plus one half (the habituation ratio) of the difference between actual and standard consumption in that previous year. This may be expressed as:

$$f_t \geqslant \bar{f_t} = \bar{f}_{t-1} + \frac{1}{2}(f_{t-1} - \bar{f}_{t-1})$$

As a consequence of this habituation ratio, the time series of standard consumption remains a nondecreasing one; but the time series of actual consumption does not necessarily have this property. This can be illustrated by means of the

118

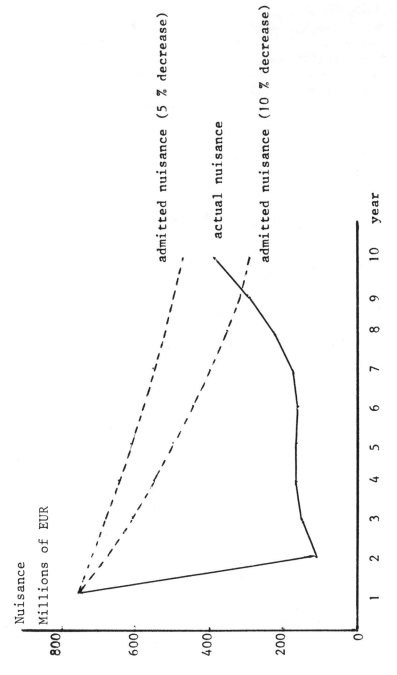

Figure 5.1

following numerical example in which standard consumption does not decrease but actual consumption does decrease from the first year onward:

$$f_0 = 100 \quad \bar{f}_0 = 100$$
$$f_1 = 120 \quad \bar{f}_1 = 100$$
$$f_2 = 118 \quad \bar{f}_2 = 110$$
$$f_3 = 116 \quad \bar{f}_3 = 114$$
$$f_4 = 115 \quad \bar{f}_4 = 115$$

In fact, the time series of actual consumption in Table 5.2.1 show this kind of pattern—except for f_2, which remains constant at its lower limit—indicating that the habituation ratio is "active" throughout.

Over a period of 10 years, the consumption of the three conventional commodities together did increase by about 25 percent. The difference of this growth rate and that of the annual wage sum (11 percent) is caused by the sharp decline in investments in later years. As a result of the lack of balance in the expansion of the capacities of the sectors, the growth of consumption is almost completely concentrated on the first commodity. These changes in the consumption pattern are a direct consequence of the application of investment model I. One of the reasons for investigating the behaviour of a second investment model is to see whether the unbalance of the growth in production and consumption can be cured by introducing a different steering device for investments.

5.3   YEAR-TO-YEAR OPTIMIZATION WITH INVESTMENT MODEL II

The main results for the year-to-year optimization with investment model II are presented in Table 5.3.1, (see Section 5.2) in exactly the same way as is done for investment model I. The comparison between the two variants reveals that the performance of the present investment model is better than that of the former. In the first place, we see that the objective function reaches a higher value. Furthermore, the lack of balance and the vanishing growth, which characterized the behaviour of the system with investment model I, are not present here.

In contrast with Table 5.2.1, Table 5.3.1 shows a modest growth of the total wage sum of about 1.5 percent per annum or 16 percent in ten years. What's more, this is a continuing growth. Deliveries for investment purposes remain possible during the whole period. The growth in capacity of the three conventional sectors was 17, 13 and 17 percent, respectively, to be compared with 33, 2 and 5 percent in Table 5.2.1. In other words, a far more balanced one. Consumption also shows a more gradual rate of growth, albeit less smoothly than the wage sum, because of 2 years with very low investments in the conventional sectors and thus relatively high consumption. Without the 50-percent habituation ratio, this would have created great difficulties.

Taking up this last remark, note that the system was in great "danger" in its second year. Because of the huge shadow price on capacity in the abatement sector in that year—not less than 30 units of account—the available investment possibilities were almost completely absorbed by investments in that sector. The situation in the second year was that the restriction regarding maximal nuisance could not be met with full capacity utilisation of the conventional sectors. Therefore, production in the second sector fell below capacity, but remained large enough to allow for some investments.

Since the second sector has a pollution coefficient of .007 and a wage share of .22 (see Table 5.1.1), an increase in the capacity of the abatement sector would indeed be very profitable. The net addition to the wage sum as a consequence of an increase of one unit of the capacity of the abatement sector, equals .956 times the ratio .22/.007 plus .07 (the wage share for the abatement sector itself), thus a little more than 30 units of account. We see in Table 5.3.1, this situation, with production in the second sector below capacity and with the same huge shadow price on the capacity of the abatement sector, is repeated in the fifth year.

From the sixth year onward, the system has practically reached the situation of balanced growth. According to the investment model II, the relative capacity expansion in each of the three conventional sectors is—under full capacity utilisation—proportional to the wage share in these sectors. Because these shares do not differ very much among themselves, growth of the conventional sectors is almost balanced. This situation will last until the claim on nuisance becomes restrictive once again. This, however, will take quite a number of years, for the abatement sector is well equipped after the enormous investment in the fifth year. The level of maximal admitted nuisance in the tenth year amounts to 473, so that actual nuisance is far below admitted nuisance. We therefore may conclude that the system can survive under the present investment model although it, too, suffers from myopia, so that its performance is no doubt greatly inferior to that under a 10-year optimization rule.

5.4   TEN-YEAR OPTIMIZATION

It is not until one observes the performance of the model under a 10-year optimization period that it becomes really clear how poor its performance is under successive 1-year optimizations. With long-term optimization, neither range conditions nor any habituation ratio or enforced investments in the abatement sec-

Table 5.4.1. Main Results for the 10-year Optimization with the Test Model.

Year	Production				Expansion of Capacity				Consumption/Nuisance				Wage Sum
	x_1	x_2	x_3	x_4	y_1	y_2	y_3	y_4	f_1	f_2	f_3	f_4	
1	28,044†	55,000	57,881†	309†	1,016	5,909	352	84	55,000	10,000	33,000	750	36,759
2	33,516	60,909	59,352	434	4,608	6,186	1,354	119	55,000	10,000	33,000	712	40,027
3	38,124	67,095	60,707	554	6,419	8,607	1,886	149	55,000	10,000	33,000	676	43,079
4	44,544	75,703	62,593	703	8,943	11,980	2,627	192	55,000	10,000	33,000	643	47,328
5	53,488	87,684	65,221	896	12,467	16,673	3,660	253	55,000	10,000	33,000	610	53,244
6	65,955	104,357	68,881	1,150	17,442	23,157	5,104	339	55,000	10,000	33,000	580	61,482
7	83,397	127,515	73,986	1,489	25,020	31,671	7,174	459	55,000	10,000	33,000	551	72,964
8	108,417	159,186	81,160	1,948	41,807	38,534	10,611	628	55,000	10,000	33,000	523	89,051
9	150,225	197,720	91,772	2,576	125,171	0	20,722	875	55,000	10,000	33,000	497	112,356
10	275,397	197,720	112,494	3,452	—	—	—	—	55,000	10,000	33,000	472	153,475

†production below capacity

121

tor are needed to keep the system alive. On the contrary, the claims on behalf of consumption and nuisance can be strengthened without any difficulties. Table 5.4.1 contains information similar to Tables 5.2.1 and 5.3.1. A quick glance at the time series reveals huge growth rates for the wage sum and actual production, but no change at all in consumption. Even the claims against this system have to be strengthened in some way or other or additional restrictions have to be incorporated, in order to prevent a too abundant and completely unrealistic growth. However, we are not going to incorporate these refinements in the test model. Analysing the performance of the full model in Chapter 6, several adaptations of the model will be submitted to a systematic analysis. At this moment we only intend to show how great the technical possibilities are under careful planning by a planning authority with a sufficiently wide horizon.

The series show two characteristics worth noticing. The first one is the incomplete use of available capacity during the first year, shown in Table 5.4.1. Three out of the four sectors produce below capacity in that year, evidently because in the long run this is advantageous in terms of the objective function. The wage sum is about 4 percent below the level attainable under full capacity utilization. But this tightening of the belt is only present during the first year. In the future everything becomes all right.

The second eye-catcher is the (rather odd) behaviour of the system after the seventh year. In Chapter 3 we have already made the distinction between the period of optimization (10 years) and the period of interest (7 years) and warned against the possibility that the results for the last years in a long-term optimization procedure might not make any sense. Therefore, the behaviour during the last 3 years is of no importance. During the period of interest, however, the system behaves quite sensibly. This supplies us with some empirical justification for the choice of a 10-year period of optimization, given a period of interest of about 7 years.

The relative expansion of capacity in the four sectors is shown in Figure 5.2. This figure reveals at a glance the difference between the period of interest and that of optimization. Investment behaviour during the last 3 years is completely senseless. Within the period of interest, however, the relative expansions of capacity show a strikingly regular trend. As these graphs show an increase in the relative additions to the capital stock, this stock must exhibit a more than exponential growth. There is no doubt that this cannot go on indefinitely. It could be redressed for example by increasing conventional consumption, as will be imposed in Chapter 6.

In the sectors that deliver investment goods, the growth of the capital stock is highest, as is to be expected of these sectors that drive the system. The recognizable "disturbance" in the first year, is probably caused by a certain disequilibrium in the chosen initial conditions for the system. This disequilibrium is easily ad-

Relative expansion of capacity for the 4 sectors of the test-model

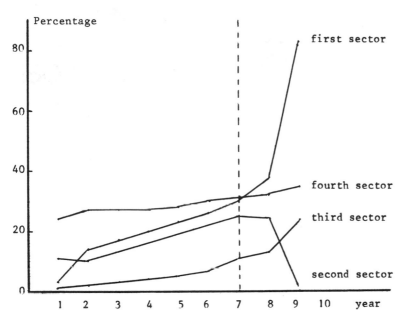

Figure 5.2

justed by the investment decisions in the first year, for we note that after the first year the increase of the growth rates of the capital stock of the sectors that deliver the investment goods is the same. The level of the growth rates, however, remains different.

6 THE FULL MODEL
Different Scenarios

6.1 INTRODUCTION

All the work that has been done in the five preceding chapters was preliminary with respect to the major aim of our study, which is to investigate the realizability of socioeconomic and political desiderata in a highly industrialized society. This last chapter will be devoted to a discussion of the results of various simulations based on the complete 22-sector model, our tool of analysis. In the next five sections we shall examine in some detail the behaviour of the system in order to distill some general principles, which will be discussed in Section 6.7. In addition we hope that some of the results of the simulations will be of practical interest.

The full model consists of 17 conventional sectors following the SOEC aggregation scheme and of 5 pollution abatement activities (see Appendix 4A). The numerical values of the model constants (the technology matrix for the Region and the matrices of depreciation and capital coefficients) as well as the initial conditions for the system, are also presented in the appendices at the end of Chapter 4. The initial conditions describe the actual situation in the Region in the base year 1965. It may be interesting to present in advance some basic data concerning the Region's economy in that year, before discussing the different scenarios we analysed.

The total wage sum for the year 1965 added up to 38.57 billion EUR.[1] The performance of the system will be compared with this point of departure. The total value of actual production was 146.5 billion EUR. The following enumeration details the expenditures in the base year.

Intermediate Deliveries:	72.4 billion EUR
Consumption:	56.2 billion EUR
Depreciation:	7.4 billion EUR
Net Capital Formation:	11.8 billion EUR
Export Surplus:	−1.3 billion EUR
Actual Production:	146.5 billion EUR

The overall wage share of actual production thus equals .26. As a further detail, we mention the ratio between consumption and the wage sum, which equals 1.46. The explanation of this apparent anomaly is that consumption covers more than just consumption by wage earners. This coefficient in particular will play an important role in this chapter, since it will be used to formulate an additional political restriction to the system.

For the sectoral details—all initial values of the system were actual sectoral values—we may refer to the appendices in Chapter 4. The results of the various simulations with the model will all be contrasted with these values.

As stated in Chapter 3, we did not use the full model to compute successive year-to-year optima. The arguments for this decision can be found in the preceding chapter. Our experiments with the full model are thus restricted to 10-year optimization. Just as we did in Chapter 5 for the test model, we started to investigate the behaviour of the full model under the simplest political restrictions imaginable. The only demands the system has to satisfy are that there shall be neither a decrease in capacity in any sector, nor a decrease in consumption of any commodity, whereas nuisance (now there are five "nuisances") has to decrease at an annual rate of at least 10 percent. This scenario (run 1) will be discussed in Section 6.2.

We see that the performance of this first variant of the model is so exuberant, that not only is it possible to render the political claims more severe in some way or other, but we even felt the need to add additional restrictions to the model in order to obtain results that are not too unrealistic. As a matter of fact, the most absurd outcome is that in all 10 years, consumption of all commodities remains at its lower limit. Mathematically this may not be surprising because—in the light of the objective function—capital accumulation is the most profitable way to use resources. But it is certainly not realistic from an economic point of view. The continual divergence between the wage sum and total consumption must be viewed as a severe imperfection of the model. However, this shortcoming of the system is easily redressed by requiring total consumption to grow every year at least as much as the wage sum. To this end, we added to the model the so-called consumption-proportionality restriction (see also Section 3.3), specified as:

$$\sum_{i=1}^{17} f_{it} \geqslant 1.46 \sum_{i=1}^{22} \xi_i x_{it} \quad (t = 1, 2, \ldots, 10)$$

in which the constant 1.46 is the ratio between consumption and wage sum in the base year. This new scenario (designated as run 2) will be discussed in Section 6.3.

The consumption-proportionality restriction does restrain the system considerably. Nevertheless, the system retains some undesirable features. There still are sectors in which the expansion of the capacity, even within the period of interest, is unacceptably high. Therefore, again a new scenario was investigated in which (besides the consumption-proportionality restriction) a limit to the annual expansion of the capacity of each sector was incorporated. The expansion was limited to 10 percent every year. This scenario (run 3) is discussed in Section 6.4.

The story threatens to become monotonous. Also, run 3 shows some disadvantages we should like to eliminate. Because of the introduction of the consumption-proportionality restriction, total consumption has to increase but the model does not contain a relation specifying a connection between the sizes of the various components of consumption. These are left completely free as long as their total obeys the proportionality restriction. The system of course searches for the cheapest way to fulfil this demand, with respect to the objective function, and the cheapest way happens to be rather nonsensical. We have tried to cure this defect of the system in a new scenario by introducing balanced growth of consumption. To be more precise, we required consumption of every commodity to increase at least at the same given percentage for all sectors and years. This scenario (run 4) is discussed in Section 6.5.

With the results and performance of run 4, we are a good deal on the way towards creating plausible time series (within the period of interest) of the capacity of the various sectors and of the consumption of the conventional goods. The growth of the output of Sector II (Energy) is 4 to 5 percent annually. Although this growth rate is not very high compared to the growth rates of other sectors, the use of energy and especially its growth are a focus of interest nowadays. Therefore, in a last scenario we investigated the implications for the system of a restriction on the use of energy. This might also serve as an example to use the model as a simple relations-bank. We will show that it is possible to keep the system alive under the additional restriction that the growth of the use of energy will not exceed 2 percent annually. The results of this scenario (run 5), which is in a certain sense the most interesting one in the sequence of scenarios is discussed in Section 6.6.

In the sequence of the five scenarios, each time more restrictions are successively added to the model, narrowing the solution space. In other words, each scenario places heavier burdens on the system than the foregoing one. Thus, we have the following chain:

Run 1   The model contains the simplest political requirements.
Run 2   The consumption-proportionality restriction is added.
Run 3   Restrictions on maximal growth of the capacity of the sectors are added.
Run 4   Restrictions on minimal growth of sectoral consumptions are added.
Run 5   Restrictions on the use of energy are added.

It is interesting to study the time paths of the variables in some detail, because the system is very astute in its pursuit of the optimum of the objective function. Also interesting to analyse is the effect each additional set of restrictions has on the size of the wage sum. In the following table the annual rates of growth of this variable are presented under the five scenarios. The most drastic changes occur at the transition from run 1 to run 2 and from run 4 to run 5. Both changes halve the average rate of growth of the wage sum. Within the period of interest the introduction of the consumption-proportionality restriction pushes the value of this key variable down from (the absurd value) 17 percent to (the very high value) 9 percent. As a consequence of introducing the restriction on the use of energy, this rate of growth falls from 6 to 3 percent.

Year	Run 1	Run 2	Run 3	Run 4	Run 5
Time Series of the Annual Rates of Growth of the Wage Sum for the Five Different Scenarios.					
1	−.01	−.01	−.01	−.10	−.10
2	.03	.02	.03	.11	.12
3	.14	.11	.06	.07	.04
4	.17	.11	.09	.08	.03
5	.20	.10	.10	.08	.03
6	.25	.10	.08	.08	.03
7	.29	.10	.08	.07	.03
8	.34	.12	.08	.07	.03
9	.38	.12	.08	.08	.03
10	.43	.11	.08	.08	.03
Average of the first 7 years[†]	.17	.09	.07	.06	.03

[†] All average growth rates in wage sum and actual production will be defined as the 1/6 power of the ratio between the actual level in the seventh year and the maximal attainable level in the first year.

All the scenarios show the same characteristic pattern in the first year: a decline of the wage sum compared to the situation in the base year 1965 due to production below capacity. Evidently, this is the price to be paid for future advantages. In the first three runs this price is relatively low, but in runs 4 and 5 it is very high indeed. The increased demands on the system on behalf of consumption put such a heavy burden on some sectors that they have to restrict their intermediate deliveries, which causes other sectors to decrease their output. This response is, of course, inevitable unless one frees the sectors involved from the constraint on consumption.

6.2 THE MODEL CONTAINING THE SIMPLEST POLITICAL REQUIREMENTS

The political requirements the system has to satisfy in this run do not restrict the system seriously; there remain ample opportunities for growth. From the consumer's point of view, however, these requirements prove to be very restrictive, because they allow consumption to remain at its lowest level during the entire period of interest. The exorbitant growth the system can realise under these (extreme) circumstances is clearly demonstrated by the time series of the (optimal) wage sum. These figures are:

Year	Wage Sum (Billions of EUR)	Growth Rate
1	38.18	−1%
2	39.22	3%
3	44.60	14%
4	52.39	17%
5	62.71	20%
6	78.13	25%
7	101.14	29%
8	135.53	34%
9	187.43	38%
10	267.82	43%

The average annual growth rate of the wage sum during the period of interest of seven years, amounted to 17 percent. It is remarkable that the full model is so much more viable than the test model (see Table 5.4.1). The two models differ somewhat with respect to pollution control and nuisance. In the test model the reduction of admitted nuisance was set at only 5 percent annually and it was assumed that in the first year already one-third of created pollution could be abated. However, these differences cannot explain the difference between the two average growth rates of the optimal wage sum. The explanation must be found in the fact that the 22-sector model, characterized by a rather great variation of its sectoral capital coefficients, has many more opportunities to find very advantageous time paths for production. This is clearly illustrated in the following table, where we see that the average growth rates of the capacity of the sectors[2] vary considerably.

	Sectoral Growth Rates			
Sector	Average Annual Growth Rate		Sector	Average Annual Growth Rate
I Agriculture	4%	X	Paper	13%
II Energy	14%	XI	Various Products	22%
III Ores	21%	XII	Building	33%
IV Minerals	28%	XIII	Commerce	10%
V Chemical Products	12%	XIV	Transport	11%
VI Metal Products	33%	XV	Money Affairs	9%
VII Means of Transport	21%	XVI	Other Market Services	2%
VIII Foods	2%	XVII	Administration	7%
IX Textiles	3%			

The time paths of sectoral actual production and the closely related expansion of sectoral capacity are presented in Tables 6.2.1 and 6.2.2, respectively. It is very interesting to scrutinize in some detail the behaviour of these variables and to examine the strange short-term relations between them, because one is compelled to realise how subtle the planning of investments has to be in order to reach the theoretical maximum.

Apart from the variation among the growth rates of sectoral production already mentioned, the most striking aspect we note in the time series of Table 6.2.1 is that in only 2 out of 17 conventional sectors, namely, Metal Products (VI) and Paper (X), actual production equals capacity all the time. The phenomenon of excess capacity at the beginning of the sequence of years, was first encountered in Chapter 5. So it is already a familiar concept, but its scope and spread are amazing. For some sectors, excess capacity exists in the second year, too, and for Administration even in the third year. However, it is not of equal

Table 6.2.1. Time Series of Actual Production in the 22 Sectors for the Model Containing the Simplest Political Requirements

Sectors	I	II	III	IV	V	VI	VII	VIII
1	7,013†	10,084†	12,816†	2,490†	6,897†	14,900	3,061†	13,252†
2	7,039†	10,322	13,879	2,206†	7,010	19,292	3,440†	13,303
3	7,220	11,336	16,274	2,900	7,594	25,295	4,366	13,464
4	7,487	12,777	19,274	4,257	8,444	31,670	5,091	13,676
5	7,873	14,693	23,644	5,775	9,567	42,149	6,364	13,975
6	8,361	17,542	30,171	8,043	11,243	57,802	8,259	14,422
7	9,144	21,786	39,918	11,432	13,744	81,172	11,089	15,092
8	10,313	28,116	54,432	16,535	17,482	115,859	15,209	16,089
9	12,040	37,685	76,694	24,218	23,086	171,793	17,734	17,534
10	13,008	53,085	130,681	26,959	31,452	357,825	17,734	18,167

Sectors	IX	X	XI	XII	XIII	XIV	XV	XVI
1	7,986†	3,410	2,937†	12,094†	17,803†	6,789†	2,559†	9,613†
2	8,020†	3,454	2,862†	9,559†	18,339	6,865	2,587	9,652†
3	8,181	3,764	3,426	13,755	19,614	7,373	2,730	9,759
4	9,404	4,202	4,402	22,645	21,162	8,128	2,937	9,901
5	8,705	4,792	5,570	32,188	23,435	9,144	3,212	10,101
6	9,153	5,673	7,315	46,447	26,831	10,587	3,622	10,399
7	9,824	6,989	9,920	67,748	31,903	12,786	4,235	10,844
8	10,824	8,953	13,837	99,903	39,425	16,073	5,150	11,507
9	12,262	11,909	19,836	148,200	50,129	21,027	6,522	12,515
10	14,147	16,149	23,138	148,200	50,129	28,003	8,402	14,429

Sectors	XVII	XVIII	XIX	XX	XXI	XXII
1	11,673†	—	—	—	—	—
2	11,683†	62	10	10	10	29†
3	12,148†	149	23	26	42	83
4	12,890	247	36	46	87	151
5	13,820	357	51	70	138	232
6	15,210	496	70	101	209	341
7	17,284	683	93	144	311	495
8	20,391	942	125	205	459	716
9	25,074	1,302	170	295	676	1,037
10	30,545	1,769	231	435	879	1,413

†Production below capacity.

Table 6.2.2. Time Series of Expansion of Capacity in the 22 Sectors for the Model Containing the Simplest Policital Requirements

Sectors	I	II	III	IV	V	VI	VII	VIII
1	–	152	919	–	–	4,392	–	3
2	170	1,013	2,395	360	584	6,003	836	161
3	266	1,441	2,999	1,356	849	6,374	724	211
4	350	1,915	4,370	1,518	1,122	10,479	1,272	298
5	523	2,848	6,527	2,268	1,675	15,652	1,895	447
6	782	4,244	9,746	3,388	2,501	23,370	2,829	669
7	1,169	6,330	14,513	5,103	3,737	34,687	4,120	996
8	1,726	9,568	22,262	7,682	5,604	55,933	2,525	1,445
9	967	15,399	53,986	2,738	8,366	186,032	–	632
10	–	–	–	–	–	–	–	–

Sectors	IX	X	XI	XII	XIII	XIV	XV	XVI
1	–	44	–	–	489	25	7	87
2	151	310	386	1,395	1,275	508	143	22
3	222	438	975	8,889	1,548	754	207	141
4	300	590	1,168	9,542	2,273	986	274	199
5	448	881	1,744	14,258	3,395	1,472	410	298
6	670	1,315	2,605	21,301	5,071	2,198	612	444
7	999	1,964	3,916	32,154	7,522	3,286	914	663
8	1,438	2,955	5,999	48,296	10,703	4,954	1,372	1,007
9	1,884	4,239	3,302	–	–	6,975	1,879	1,914
10	–	–	–	–	–	–	–	–

132

Sectors	XVII	XVIII	XIX	XX	XXI	XXII
1	1,160	62	10	10	10	83
2	–	87	12	16	31	–
3	–	97	13	19	44	67
4	930	109	15	23	51	80
5	1,389	139	18	31	71	109
6	2,074	186	23	43	101	153
7	3,106	259	32	61	147	221
8	4,683	359	44	90	216	320
9	5,471	467	60	139	203	376
10	–	538	–	–	–	–

importance in all sectors. If we neglect the figures below 1 percent, relative excess capacity appears to be concentrated in seven sectors. These sectors and the corresponding data are:

	Sectoral Excess Capacity		
Sector	Year 1	Year 2	Year 3
III Ores	1%	—	—
IV Minerals	2%	13%	—
V Chemical Products	2%	—	—
VII Means of Transport	13%	3%	—
XI Various Products	3%	6%	—
XII Building	2%	23%	—
XVII Administration	—	9%	6%
Total	1%	3%	0%

The largest divergences occur in the first year in the Means of Transport sector and in the second year in the Minerals and Building sectors. In three sectors— Minerals, Various Products and Building—actual production in the second year is below its level in the first year, notwithstanding an overall increase of the wage sum of 3 percent.

Table 6.2.2 shows that excess capacity of a sector in a certain year does not at all exclude expansion of the capacity of that sector. In the first year, there was expansion in 7 out of the 15 sectors with excess capacity. However, sectors that show excess capacity also in the second year do not expand anymore. There is but one unexplainable exception, the Administration sector. On the other hand, in the ninth year, production at capacity level does not imply expansion of that capacity. The ninth year is the last year in which expansion of capacity does make sense to the system. It is therefore rather peculiar that the system expands the capacity of one of the abatement sectors in the tenth year. It is one of the few examples of the solution process giving a nonzero value to one of the variables, which is difficult to explain. Apart from the few details we have mentioned, the qualitative investment behaviour of the system is rather lucid. In nearly all sectors, relative expansion of capacity increases with time during the period of interest, albeit at different levels and at different accelerations, reflecting the differences in the average annual growth rates of capacity.

We shall not present a detailed table containing the time paths of sectoral consumption and nuisance. For the present scenario, such information is superfluous because consumption remains at its minimal level in all conventional sectors. The nuisances are decreasing, but never more rapidly than is required by the corresponding restrictions.

Some Remarks on Shadow Prices

Recall that there are four types of restrictions incorporated in the model: the Leontief, the disinvestment, the capacity and the political ones. Therefore, there are also four types of shadow prices, but only those on the political restrictions are of practical interest.

The shadow price on a restriction represents the increase of the optimal value of the objective function that would result if the corresponding restriction were weakened by one unit. Now weakening the Leontief restrictions or the capacity restrictions is not possible in the context of the model. These restrictions are technical data and not subject to political considerations. This is true to a lesser degree for the disinvestment restrictions. Zero investments in a sector, sometimes to be noticed, imply that in that year the disinvestment restriction is binding and that it will have a nonzero shadow price. It is interesting to see that these shadow prices are relatively small in comparison with those on the political restrictions. This is to be understood because any disinvestment—however advantageous it may be at the moment—makes extra investments at a future time necessary. So these advantages are of a marginal character, and we shall omit this type of shadow price from further discussion.

The most interesting shadow prices, therefore, are those on the political restrictions. Their behaviour in the course of time is given in Table 6.2.3. The political restrictions are different from the other types of restrictions in the sense that they are the product of a social decision process. While considering the taking of a certain decision, the consequence for the objective function of making that decision must be one of the prime considerations, and it is precisely this consequence that is measured by the shadow price. It is therefore important to realise that the shadow prices often are far from negligible. As shown in Table 6.2.3 they do indeed sometimes reach enormous values, especially in the abatement sectors. One may wonder, for example, whether the control of water pollution is a justifiable proposition if one realises that 1 million units of Private Waste Water Treatment (Sector XIX) has an opportunity cost of 350 million units. On the other hand of course, one has to take into account that this first model examined in this section, is still far from realistic. In this version, where final consumption is allowed to remain stationary, the actual meaning of such an opportunity cost is not immediately evident.

The general pattern of the time series of shadow prices shown in Table 6.2.3, is that they decline towards zero at the end of the period of optimization. This trend, existing in every sector, is easily understood. It merely reflects that as the remaining time decreases, the opportunity loss caused by a certain decision also decreases.

Obviously, the present version of the model has only illustrative value. One perhaps trivial conclusion to be drawn from this run is that pollution abatement certainly does not prevent economic growth.

Table 6.2.3. Time Series of Shadow Prices on Political Restrictions for the Model Containing the Simplest Political Requirements

Sectors	I	II	III	IV	V	VI	VII	VIII
1	65.61	114.75	†	55.97	89.10	108.79	68.05	57.35
2	59.13	109.47		50.16	84.45	48.12	52.94	54.38
3	49.17	66.15		38.78	46.38	25.70	37.22	38.95
4	31.73	43.94		22.84	28.00	15.52	22.12	25.12
5	20.07	27.88		13.89	17.28	9.12	13.32	15.70
6	12.38	17.17		8.14	10.32	5.05	7.68	9.53
7	7.34	10.16		4.49	5.84	2.53	4.13	5.53
8	4.09	5.63		2.24	3.05	1.06	1.98	2.98
9	2.02	2.76		0.93	1.37	0.29	0.76	1.41
10	0.77	1.02		0.27	0.46	–	–	0.51

Sectors	IX	X	XI	XII	XIII	XIV	XV	XVI
1	39.87	57.93	46.12	43.74	36.37	71.41	66.14	153.64
2	38.96	57.93	41.17	35.59	33.22	66.12	61.92	148.06
3	28.44	32.23	30.14	24.70	21.33	44.08	51.37	142.01
4	17.66	20.12	18.37	15.20	14.19	30.95	41.64	113.87
5	10.56	12.16	11.04	8.94	8.52	18.81	25.67	73.76
6	6.00	7.00	6.33	4.96	4.90	11.18	14.91	46.28
7	3.15	3.75	3.37	2.50	2.62	6.30	8.10	28.06
8	1.44	1.79	1.59	1.06	1.25	3.27	3.94	16.05
9	0.51	0.68	0.59	0.30	0.48	1.46	1.57	8.21
10	0.09	0.16	0.14	–	–	0.55	0.41	3.22

Sectors	XVII	XVIII	XIX	XX	XXI	XXII
1	74.28	—	—	—	—	—
2	69.06	99.68	356.01	187.45	263.75	86.11
3	62.69	79.48	152.42	78.78	119.73	66.57
4	58.76	58.65	78.73	39.85	65.41	50.81
5	38.14	39.01	50.80	25.26	41.95	31.36
6	23.43	24.95	32.33	15.82	26.52	19.71
7	13.81	15.51	19.97	9.55	16.24	12.04
8	7.61	9.16	11.67	5.43	9.40	6.99
9	3.70	4.89	6.16	2.74	4.88	3.70
10	1.36	2.09	2.52	1.06	1.98	1.87

† Since sector III (Ores) does not deliver goods for final consumption, no shadow prices are reported in this column.

6.3 CONSUMPTION-PROPORTIONALITY

Referring to Section 3.2 and to the introduction to the present chapter for the mathematical formulation of the consumption-proportionality restriction, we repeat that this modification purports to keep the ratio of total consumption to the total wage sum equal to that in the base year. In a democratic society it is reasonable to require that an increase in wages has to be accompanied by an increase in consumption. One might consider this restriction too rigorous, because one should like to incorporate some increase in the saving ratio. But on the other hand, growing wages together with a constant level of total consumption will be unacceptable, and the consumption-proportionality assumption is the simplest way to force the system to provide for additional consumption goods.

This newly added restriction strongly influences the performance of the system. The time path of the optimal annual wage sum becomes less absurd than in the first run. Compared to the preceding case, the increase of the annual wage sum is halved from 17 to 9 percent. In the first and second years, when the system is starting up, growth is slow. After the second year, the growth rate is more or less constant at a level of about 11 percent. Of course, the decline in the growth of the wage sum is reflected in the growth of output. A quick glance at Table 6.3.1 confirms this statement, insofar that most of the sectoral growth rates of production are below those found in the first run. There exist, however, some striking exceptions, which are indicated by means of an arrow in the following table of sectoral growth rates.

	Sectoral Growth Rates			
Sector	Average Annual Growth Rate	Sector		Average Annual Growth Rate
I Agriculture	6% ↑	X	Paper	10%
II Energy	7%	XI	Various Products	7%
III Ores	7%	XII	Building	7%
IV Minerals	7%	XIII	Commerce	23% ↑
V Chemical Products	4%	XIV	Transport	6%
VI Metal Products	13%	XV	Money Affairs	6%
VII Means of Transport	10%	XVI	Other Market Services	1%
VIII Foods	4% ↑	XVII	Administration	2%
IX Textiles	2%			

In the Agriculture and Foods sectors, the growth rates are higher but remain within reasonable bounds. In the Commerce sector, however, the growth rate is more than doubled from 10 to 23 percent, this sector now being extremely expansive. We shall return to this phenomenon when the time series of consumption is illustrated in Table 6.3.3.

Another aspect of the time series of sectoral production, shown in Table 6.3.1, relates to the structure and size of sectoral excess capacity. Practically the same sectors as in Section 6.2 exhibit this trait. Excess capacity now lasts until the fourth year. Neglecting again the sectors in which the difference between capacity and actual production is below 1 percent, the following table shows relative excess capacity for the relevant sectors.

Sectoral Excess Capacity				
Sector	Year 1	Year 2	Year 3	Year 4
IV Minerals	—	13%	—	—
V Chemical Products	1%	—	—	—
VII Means of Transport	10%	—	—	—
XI Various Products	3%	6%	—	—
XII Building	—	22%	11%	—
XVI Other Market Services	—	2%	1%	—
XVII Administration	—	8%	5%	2%
Total	1%	3%	1%	0%

The Means of Transport sector in the first year, Minerals in the second year and Building in the second and third years, are affected the most. Compared to the situation for the first run, the structure and size of excess capacity is remarkably insensitive to the introduction of the consumption-proportionality restriction. The main consequence is a small shift in time.

The expansion of the capacity of the sectors (see Table 6.3.2) shows (already within the period of interest of 7 years) a pattern that is appreciably less regular than the one depicted in Table 6.2.2. Especially the Building (XII) and Commerce (XIII) sectors should be mentioned because of the extreme variation of their yearly expansion. There is no doubt that the proportionality restriction has forced the system into more indirect paths to reach its optimal value.

The way the proportionality restriction acts upon consumption is quite unexpected. From Table 6.3.3, containing the time series of shadow prices on the political restrictions (i.e., the restrictions that prevent sectoral consumption to decrease), we can see that all shadow prices in the conventional sectors are non-

Table 6.3.1. Time Series of Actual Production in the 22 Sectors for the Model with Consumption Proportionality.

Sectors	I	II	III	IV	V	VI	VII	VIII
1	7,020†	10,114†	12,866†	2,528†	6,915†	14,900	3,174†	13,258†
2	7,088	10,287	13,551	2,208†	6,975†	17,855	3,823	13,379
3	7,562	11,081	14,512	2,456†	7,326	19,993	4,527	14,039
4	8,109	11,988	15,484	2,852	7,728	21,850	5,011	14,793
5	8,653	12,889	16,459	3,241	8,129	23,726	5,519	15,543
6	9,236	13,853	17,584	3,600	8,558	26,138	6,145	16,352
7	9,902	14,977	19,135	3,875	9,058	30,511	6,403	17,289
8	10,175	16,427	21,622	5,719	9,903	34,090	6,403	17,474
9	10,363	18,021	26,622	6,176	10,796	50,529	6,679	17,644
10	10,468	19,707	32,496	6,474	11,708	70,770	6,679	17,712

Sectors	IX	X	XI	XII	XIII	XIV	XV	XVI
1	7,993†	3,408†	2,964†	12,360	17,850	6,807†	2,564†	9,616†
2	8,028†	3,468	2,852†	9,687†	19,210	6,860	2,592†	9,649†
3	8,177	3,878	3,119	10,963†	26,269	7,295	2,762	9,761†
4	8,343	4,348	3,472	13,333	34,313	7,801	2,958	9,886
5	8,509	4,816	3,822	15,642	42,324	8,305	3,153	10,010
6	8,688	5,319	4,174	17,656	50,951	8,842	3,361	10,146
7	8,885	5,905	4,499	18,857	60,969	9,456	3,602	10,310
8	9,098	6,338	5,684	31,586	62,159	10,245	3,813	10,438
9	9,313	6,807	6,217	33,046	63,295	10,998	4,022	10,631
10	9,518	7,269	6,576	33,046	63,295	11,757	4,226	10,839

Sectors	XVII	XVIII	XIX	XX	XXI	XXII
1	11,691†	–	–	–	–	–
2	11,675†	62	10	9	9	30†
3	11,990†	149	25	24	31	94
4	12,375†	234	39	39	55	161
5	12,757	315	53	53	78	227
6	13,155	395	66	67	101	294
7	13,588	476	81	81	122	366
8	14,436	557	91	99	170	430
9	15,038	634	102	117	199	484
10	15,633	706	113	136	226	535

†Production below capacity.

EMPIRICAL INVESTIGATIONS

Table 6.3.2. Time Series of Expansion of Capacity in the 22 Sectors for the
Model with Consumption Proportionality.

Sector	I	II	III	IV	V	VI	VII	VIII
1	38	117	591	–	–	2,955	293	79
2	473	794	961	–	316	2,138	703	659
3	546	906	972	312	402	1,856	483	753
4	544	900	975	388	401	1,875	508	750
5	582	964	1,124	358	428	2,411	626	808
6	665	1,123	1,551	275	500	4,373	258	937
7	273	1,450	2,487	1,843	844	3,579	–	185
8	187	1,593	5,000	456	893	16,439	275	170
9	104	1,686	5,874	298	911	20,240	–	67
10	–	–	–	–	–	–	–	–

Sector	IX	X	XI	XII	XIII	XIV	XV	XVI
1	–	58	–	–	1,360	20	182	236
2	147	410	79	–	7,059	434	–	–
3	165	469	353	973	8,044	506	195	–
4	165	467	349	2,309	8,010	504	194	124
5	179	502	352	2,013	8,626	537	208	135
6	196	586	325	1,201	10,018	613	240	164
7	212	433	1,185	12,728	1,189	797	211	127
8	215	469	532	1,460	1,136	744	208	193
9	205	461	359	–	–	759	204	208
10	–	–	–	–	–	–	–	–

Sector	XVII	XVIII	XIX	XX	XXI	XXII
1	887	62	10	9	9	94
2	–	86	14	14	22	–
3	–	85	14	14	24	67
4	139	80	13	14	22	65
5	397	79	13	13	22	67
6	433	81	14	14	21	72
7	847	80	10	17	48	63
8	601	76	10	18	28	54
9	595	72	10	18	26	50
10	–	–	–	–	–	–

Table 6.3.3. Time Series of Shadow Prices on the Political Restrictions for the Model with Consumption Proportionality.

Sector	I	II	III	IV	V	VI	VII	VIII
1	10.06	16.14	†	5.15	8.39	14.21	11.80	6.62
2	8.51	15.22		3.93	7.43	4.22	9.14	5.75
3	6.34	12.21		3.67	6.75	2.15	5.34	4.08
4	5.09	9.54		3.54	5.06	1.34	3.66	3.26
5	4.08	7.48		2.47	3.70	0.79	2.47	2.59
6	3.27	5.75		1.74	2.71	0.39	1.65	2.05
7	2.51	4.22		1.17	1.89	0.13	1.03	1.56
8	1.91	3.01		0.78	1.30	0.01	0.56	1.19
9	1.39	2.03		0.52	0.87	—	0.38	0.89
10	0.76	1.03		0.27	0.45	—	—	0.51

Sector	IX	X	XI	XII	XIII	XIV	XV	XVI
1	3.47	6.39	4.42	3.79	11.29	10.25	15.59	29.64
2	3.24	6.39	3.30	1.65	—	9.16	15.13	28.66
3	2.80	3.79	2.99	1.22	—	8.68	13.10	28.87
4	1.89	2.69	2.04	1.09	—	6.18	10.82	29.21
5	1.25	1.89	1.37	0.65	—	4.49	8.61	25.00
6	0.78	1.26	0.90	0.31	—	3.19	5.87	19.31
7	0.44	0.78	0.54	0.08	—	2.18	3.70	14.19
8	0.25	0.48	0.34	—	0.05	1.46	2.15	10.02
9	0.17	0.31	0.23	—	0.12	0.90	1.12	6.58
10	0.09	0.16	0.13	—	—	0.53	0.41	3.23

Sector	XVII	XVIII	XIX	XX	XXI	XXII
1	13.11	—	—	—	—	—
2	12.35	26.21	67.78	36.14	52.28	24.87
3	12.07	21.98	36.17	20.08	30.38	20.81
4	11.97	17.85	26.54	14.42	22.33	16.81
5	11.94	14.38	19.40	10.32	16.43	12.22
6	9.01	11.26	14.88	7.68	12.46	9.04
7	6.44	8.43	11.03	5.50	9.11	6.54
8	4.43	6.05	7.82	3.74	6.35	4.59
9	2.86	4.03	5.11	2.31	4.05	2.75
10	1.36	2.07	2.54	1.07	1.99	1.74

†Since Sector III (Ores) does not deliver goods for final consumption, no shadow prices are reported in this column.

zero in the first year. Therefore, all these restrictions are binding; consumption in all sectors is at its minimal level in the first year. This implies that the proportionality restriction is not binding. From the second to the seventh year on, all shadow prices remain nonzero with one exception. This means that consumption remains at its minimum in all sectors, except for the Commerce sector (XIII). In those six successive years, the Commerce sector provides all the additional output required as a consequence of the introduction of the proportionality restriction. Maybe this is the kind of society we are gradually drifting into, but for the moment it might be better to introduce restrictions preventing this extreme type of behaviour of the system.

There is another interesting aspect of Table 6.3.3 that arrests the attention immediately, namely, the lower level of the shadow prices as compared to those in Table 6.2.3. This, of course, is due to the presence of the proportionality restriction. Shadow prices indicate the consequences for the optimal wage sum of a one-unit change in the right-hand side of a political restriction, but any increase in the wage sum would by necessity lead to an increase in consumption, just because of the proportionality restriction. This enforced increase has to be compensated by a decrease of (possible) investments, which tends to depress the value of the objective function, so that the net result (the shadow price) becomes smaller to the same extent.

Because the system will satisfy the consumption-proportionality restriction in the cheapest way possible and there is quite a lot of freedom in this respect, it is to be expected that the shadow prices on this restriction are only modest. The following series were found:

Year 1:	0.00	Year 6:	1.13
Year 2:	2.94	Year 7:	0.87
Year 3:	2.69	Year 8:	0.63
Year 4:	1.91	Year 9:	0.30
Year 5:	1.49	Year 10:	0.00

However, one should realise that especially up from the third year, the effect of the restriction nevertheless was an enormous increase in total consumption.

6.4 LIMITED GROWTH OF SECTORAL CAPACITY

In this run of the model, an additional set of restrictions is introduced again. The maximal admitted growth of capacity of the conventional sectors is put at 10 percent per annum. Since this restriction is meant to hold for every sector and every year, not less than 170 restrictions on the expansion of capacity are added to the system.

The influence of this set of restrictions on the time path of the annual wage sum is not as great as has been the case with the introduction of the consumption-proportionality restriction, but it is not negligible. The average annual rate of growth of wages in the period of interest now becomes 7 percent, to be compared with 9 percent in the preceding section. Although this decline in the growth rate of wages is relatively small, the performance of the system is altered considerably.

At first sight it seems that only the growth rates of the capacity of the Metal Products and Commerce sectors—which were over 10 percent—have to fall. However, limiting the expansion in these sectors and remembering that the Commerce sector had to deliver the additional consumption goods to satisfy the proportionality restriction, it becomes obvious that the growth rates of other sectors have to rise. Referring to Tables 6.4.1 and 6.4.2, containing the time series of sectoral production and expansion of capacity, we see that this is just what happens. Besides the Metal Products and Commerce sectors, for which the growth rates fall to their upper limits, the rates for the Textiles, Various Products, Building and Money Affairs sectors rise till they meet their upper bounds too. The average annual growth rates per sector are included in the following table; the arrows (↑) indicate increases with respect to the corresponding list in Section 6.3.

		Sectoral Growth Rates			
	Sector	*Average Annual Growth Rate*		*Sector*	*Average Annual Growth Rate*
I	Agriculture	6%	X	Paper	10%
II	Energy	5%	XI	Various Products	10% ↑
III	Ores	6%	XII	Building	10% ↑
IV	Minerals	9% ↑	XIII	Commerce	10%
V	Chemical Products	5% ↑	XIV	Transport	6%
VI	Metal Products	10%	XV	Money Affairs	10% ↑
VII	Means of Transport	7%	XVI	Other Market Services	1%
VIII	Foods	4%	XVII	Administration	3% ↑
IX	Textiles	10% ↑			

The newly added restrictions tend to reduce the variation among the sectoral growth rates, but note that those of the slow-growing Agriculture, Foods and (especially) Other Market Services sectors, do not show any upward tendency. Under the new circumstances, their average growth rates remain unaffected. As a consequence, these sectors are absent in the array of sectors that deliver the required additional consumption goods to compensate for the reduction of the

Table 6.4.1. Time Series of Actual Production in the 22 Sectors for the Model with Consumption Proportionality and Restricted Maximal Capacity Growth (10%).

Sector	I	II	III	IV	V	VI	VII	VIII
1	7,023†	10,113†	12,853†	2,525†	6,916†	14,900	3,113†	13,259†
2	7,062	10,279	13,231	2,383†	6,976†	16,390	3,530	13,323
3	7,347	10,723	13,783	2,441†	7,233	18,029	3,657	13,638
4	7,740	11,378	14,678	2,814†	7,736	19,831	4,023	13,927
5	8,080	12,225	15,871	3,491	8,258	21,815	4,425	14,216
6	8,874	12,980	16,865	3,840	8,737	23,996	4,868	15,407
7	9,762	13,840	17,948	4,224	9,611	26,396	5,355	16,738
8	10,165	14,670	19,116	4,646	10,125	29,035	5,890	17,106
9	10,606	15,552	20,399	5,111	10,687	31,939	6,479	17,510
10	11,091	16,493	21,807	5,622	11,277	35,133	7,127	17,952

Sector	IX	X	XI	XII	XIII	XIV	XV	XVI
1	8,030	3,410	2,953†	12,337†	17,850	6,806†	2,580	9,617†
2	8,020†	3,485†	2,923†	11,091†	18,521†	6,876	2,838	9,652†
3	8,809†	4,126	3,031†	11,182†	21,598	7,110	3,121	9,717†
4	10,687	4,538	3,763†	13,442†	23,758	7,462	3,433	9,793
5	11,756	4,992	4,450	17,891†	26,134	8,208	3,777	9,844
6	12,932	5,491	4,895	19,905	28,747	9,029	4,155	9,977†
7	14,225	6,041	5,385	21,896	31,622	9,932	4,570	10,081
8	15,648	6,645	5,924	24,086	34,784	10,842	5,027	10,182
9	17,213	7,309	6,516	26,494	38,263	11,631	5,530	10,292
10	18,934	8,040	7,168	29,144	42,098	12,304	6,083	10,410

146

Sector	XVII	XVIII	XIX	XX	XXI	XXII
1	11,730	—	—	—	—	—
2	12,577†	64	10	9	11	30
3	12,767†	153	24	21	29	72†
4	13,090†	256	36	34	55	118†
5	13,531†	347	48	43	85	169†
6	13,878†	442	64	61	108	215
7	14,259	544	80	74	133	261
8	14,648	632	92	86	156	308
9	15,074	722	103	98	180	355
10	15,538	816	115	111	205	404

† Production below capacity.

147

Table 6.4.2. Time Series of Expansion of Capacity in the 22 Sectors for the Model with Consumption Proportionality and Restricted Maximal Capacity Growth (10%).

Sector	I	II	III	IV	V	VI	VII	VIII
1	12	109	271	82	–	1,490	–	23
2	284	443	551	262	223	1,639	127	315
3	393	654	895	288	503	1,802	365	289
4	339	847	1,192	317	522	1,983	402	288
5	794	755	993	349	479	2,181	442	1,191
6	887	859	1,082	384	873	2,399	486	1,330
7	402	829	1,168	422	513	2,639	535	368
8	441	882	1,282	464	561	2,903	589	403
9	484	940	1,408	511	589	3,193	647	442
10	–	–	–	–	–	–	–	–

Sector	IX	X	XI	XII	XIII	XIV	XV	XVI
1	803	341	304	1,236	1,785	36	258	70
2	883	375	334	1,359	1,963	234	283	–
3	971	412	367	1,495	2,159	351	312	72
4	1,068	453	404	1,645	2,375	746	343	91
5	1,175	499	445	1,809	2,613	820	377	112
6	1,293	549	489	1,990	2,874	902	415	84
7	1,422	604	538	2,189	3,162	910	457	101
8	1,564	664	592	2,408	3,478	788	502	109
9	1,721	730	651	2,649	3,826	673	553	117
10	–	–	–	–	–	–	–	–

Sector	XVII	XVIII	XIX	XX	XXI	XXII
1	1,173	64	10	9	11	30
2	744	88	13	11	17	117
3	389	103	12	13	26	35
4	168	90	12	13	29	10
5	54	95	15	12	23	20
6	–	101	16	13	24	46
7	389	87	11	11	23	46
8	425	90	11	12	23	47
9	463	93	11	12	25	49
10	–	–	–	–	–	–

output of the Commerce sector. We shall return to this subject when illustrating the time paths of final consumption in Table 6.4.3.

The quantitative aspect of the phenomenon of sectoral excess capacity is examined next. The following table contains the sectors with a relative excess capacity of more than 1 percent. Not only is the list of sectors involved longer than that of the preceding scenarios, but it also appears that (within the period of interest of 7 years) the problem becomes a chronic one; all capacity is in use only in the seventh year. Optimizing total employment over a 10-years period, with some side restrictions to ensure an "acceptable" shape of the time series of production and consumption, causes severe and lasting excess capacity in some sectors. In actual practice, this would not be an acceptable feature of a production plan. But it has to be realised that the only way to eliminate this trait is either to drop the requirement that the existing capacity of a given sector cannot be reduced, or to introduce more restrictions, or to use a multicriteria objective function. It is to be stressed that these last two alternatives reduce the optimum, whereas the first one is certain to meet determined opposition.

	Sector	*Sectoral Excess Capacity*					
		Year 1	*Year 2*	*Year 3*	*Year 4*	*Year 5*	*Year 6*
IV	Minerals	–	9%	15%	11%	–	
V	Chemical Products	1%	–	–	–	–	–
VII	Means of Transport	12%	–	–		–	–
IX	Textiles	–	9%	9%	–	–	–
X	Paper	–	–	7%	–	–	–
XI	Various Products	3%	13%	18%	7%	–	–
XII	Building	–	18%	25%	18%	1%	–
XIII	Commerce	–	6%	–	–	–	
XVII	Administration	–	3%	6%	7%	5%	3%
	Total	1%	4%	4%	3%	0%	0%

Next to the Minerals, Means of Transport and Building sectors, which were already noted as problem sectors in the two preceding sections, now also Textiles and Various Products encounter these difficulties. It is the requirement of maximal sectoral growth of 10 percent per year that is largely responsible for these troubles. It then becomes natural to ask the question of how expensive this claim is. Because the sectoral growth rates are frequently equal to their upper limit—actually, this occurs in 84 out of 170 possible cases—much information about these restrictions is available in the form of shadow prices. Their sizes

Table 6.4.3. Time Series of Final Consumption in the 22 Sectors for the Model with Consumption Proportionality and Restricted Maximal Capacity Growth (10%).

Sectors	I	II	III	IV	V	VI	VII	VIII
1	2,130	2,180	—	160	1,060	1,600	1,100	9,260
2	2,130	2,180	—	160	1,060	1,600	1,100	9,260
3	2,130	2,180	—	160	1,060	1,600	1,100	9,260
4	2,130	2,180	—	160	1,060	1,600	1,100	9,260
5	2,130	2,180	—	160	1,060	1,600	1,100	9,260
6	2,130	2,180	—	160	1,060	1,781	1,126	9,964
7	2,130	2,180	—	177	1,331	3,060	1,288	10,746
8	2,130	2,180	—	218	1,331	3,831	1,475	10,746
9	2,130	2,180	—	263	1,331	4,702	1,687	10,746
10	2,130	2,180	—	263	1,331	4,702	1,687	10,746

Sectors	IX	X	XI	XII	XIII	XIV	XV	XVI
1	4,100	610	1,360	240	11,540	1,590	750	9,290
2	4,100	610	1,360	240	11,945	1,590	867	9,290
3	4,559	913	1,360	240	14,565	1,590	961	9,290
4	5,680	1,016	1,700	2,334	16,106	1,590	1,057	9,290
5	6,274	1,119	1,856	6,254	17,712	1,871	1,154	9,290
6	6,948	1,258	1,963	7,807	19,608	2,282	1,271	9,290
7	7,688	1,401	2,104	7,868	21,845	2,730	1,400	9,290
8	8,510	1,596	2,262	9,211	24,290	3,189	1,549	9,290
9	9,414	1,813	2,438	10,686	26,991	3,496	1,715	9,290
10	9,414	1,813	2,438	18,162	26,991	3,656	1,715	9,290

Sectors	XVII	XVIII	XIX	XX	XXI	XXII
1	9,266	539	94	84	98	247
2	10,043	485	85	76	88	223
3	10,043	437	76	68	79	200
4	10,043	393	69	61	71	180
5	10,043	354	62	55	64	162
6	10,043	318	55	50	57	145
7	10,043	286	50	45	52	131
8	10,043	258	45	40	46	118
9	10,043	232	40	36	42	106
10	10,043	209	36	32	38	96

prove to be rather small, less than 2 EUR, which indicates that the restrictions are not too prohibitive. Sector VI is the exception, with shadow prices that are much higher during the first 3 years. This sector, Metal Products, actually is not well equipped in the first years. Widening the upper bound on the growth of its capacity for the first years, would benefit the performance of the system appreciably.

Some Remarks on Consumption

We now present the time series of sectoral consumption themselves (see Table 6.4.3) instead of those of the shadow prices on the political restrictions, because these series are very interesting and the behaviour of the system can be better understood in this way.

In the base year, we observed that only 7 out of 17 sectors were responsible for the delivery of 85 percent of the goods and services for final consumption. These sectors and their relative importance as suppliers of consumption goods are:

I	Agriculture	2.02 billion EUR, or 4% of total consumption
II	Energy	2.18 billion EUR, or 4% of total consumption
VIII	Foods	9.26 billion EUR, or 16% of total consumption
IX	Textiles	4.10 billion EUR, or 7% of total consumption
XIII	Commerce	11.54 billion EUR, or 21% of total consumption
XVI	Other Market Services	9.29 billion EUR, or 17% of total consumption
XVII	Administration	9.23 billion EUR, or 16% of total consumption

In Section 6.3 we saw that the necessary increase in total consumption enforced by the proportionality restriction, was solely provided by the Commerce sector. In the seventh year for instance, the value of "services" consumed, amounted to more than 40 billion EUR. In the present section, under the newly added restrictions on expansion of the capacity, the necessary increase in total consumption no longer consists of the output of the Commerce sector only, but it is produced by 13 out of the 17 sectors. Unfortunately, one finds that of the seven main sectors mentioned before, only Textiles and Commerce show a marked increase in consumption, whereas for the other five main sectors the increase of consumption was only slight or even zero. The increase of consumption delivered by the Paper, Various Products, Transport and Money Affairs sectors might be meaningful in practise; the strongly rising consumption of the output of the Building sector is not. In the base year, this kind of consumption (240 million EUR) was a very small proportion of total consumption. Normally, the output of the Building sector has to be invested in Sector XVI (i.e., the leasing of real estate) because it is not the house but its continuing "service" (the roof above one's head) that is the consumption good in reality.

Although the performance of the present run brings us quite a step ahead towards an acceptable performance of the system regarding the time paths of sectoral consumption, we must conclude that the run described in this section is still far from satisfactory. Certainly more balance in sectoral output is achieved, but more balance in sectoral consumption evidently has to be secured in another way.

6.5 MINIMAL GROWTH OF SECTORAL CONSUMPTION

The results of the run described in the preceding section revealed that even under some stringent additional restrictions, considerable economic growth was possible. The worst feature of the performance of the system was the large variation in the growth rates of sectoral consumption, which entails major changes in the consumption pattern. It might be that, for instance, because of political considerations, the issue of economic growth or the reduction of unemployment has to prevail over the composition of the basket of consumers' goods, but the unbalance as described in Section 6.4, is too strong. Therefore, in this section we shall enforce a more balanced growth of sectoral consumption by introducing restrictions containing lower bounds on their annual growth rates.

Note that this modification does not imply the incorporation into the model of new restrictions. It suffices simply to change the original political requirement that consumption should at least equal last year's level, into the requirement that consumption should at least rise at a given annual rate. Experience with this modification of the model showed that only a small percentage rise was attainable. A 2-percent growth rate of sectoral consumption already proved to be infeasible. A 1-percent growth rate could be supported, and in this section we shall present the results of a run of the model in which the political restrictions on conventional consumption are changed into:

$$f_{it} \geqslant 1.01 f_{i(t-1)} \quad (i = 1, 2, \ldots, 17; \quad t = 1, 2, \ldots, 10)$$

It is amazing that this rather rigorous curtailment of the system's freedom has such a small effect on the maximum value of the objective function. In the seventh year, the wage sum amounted to 55.1 billion EUR, to be compared with 58.4 billion EUR in Section 6.4. Since the initial value of the wage sum equals 38.6 billion EUR, the average annual rate of growth of wages declines from 7 percent to 6 percent only. This "price" for a (more) balanced consumption is certainly not a very high one.

The decline in the growth of wages finds its counterpart in a decrease of the growth of production. The growth rates of sectoral productive capacity become smaller in general (compare Tables 6.5.1 and 6.5.2). We see in the list of the

Table 6.5.1. Time Series of Actual Production in the 22 Sectors for the Model with Consumption Proportionality, Restricted Maximal Capacity Growth (10%) and Minimal Growth in Consumption (1%).

Sector	I	II	III	IV	V	VI	VII	VIII
1	6,991†	9,492†	11,539†	1,720†	6,527†	12,664†	2,871†	13,296†
2	7,220	10,236	13,031	2,253†	6,956†	16,151	3,374†	13,537
3	7,516	10,753	13,733	2,492†	7,217	17,738†	3,665	13,918
4	7,823	11,399	14,674	2,959	7,583	19,542	3,922	14,265
5	8,294	12,049	15,537	3,255	8,062	21,497	4,256	14,690
6	8,740	12,749	16,494	3,581	8,536	23,646	4,682	15,122
7	9,179	13,485	17,520	3,939	8,997	26,011	5,150	15,571
8	9,652	14,265	18,645	4,333	9,500	28,612	5,665	16,052
9	10,163	15,105	19,881	4,719	10,046	31,473	6,232	16,569
10	10,715	16,004	21,190	5,140	10,607	34,621	6,567	17,124

Sector	IX	X	XI	XII	XIII	XIV	XV	XVI
1	7,952†	3,203†	2,439†	6,840†	17,298†	6,455†	2,483†	9,650
2	8,128	3,435	2,868†	10,160†	18,205†	6,831†	2,602	9,818
3	8,275†	3,652	3,092†	11,559†	20,827	7,100	2,706	9,974
4	8,456†	3,894†	3,678	14,552†	22,910	7,443	2,826	10,137
5	10,459†	4,163†	4,046	16,284†	25,201	7,783	2,951	10,308
6	11,901	4,861	4,450	18,096	27,721	8,151	3,085	10,488
7	13,091	5,348	4,895	19,905	30,493	8,721	3,226	10,672
8	14,400	5,882	5,385	21,896	33,543	9,138	3,540	10,865
9	15,840	6,471	5,924	24,086	36,897	9,588	3,803	11,067
10	17,424	7,118	6,516	26,494	40,587	10,076	4,183	11,297

Sector	XVII	XVIII	XIX	XX	XXI	XXII
1	11,403†	–	–	–	–	–
2	11,836	82	12	14	25	45
3	12,140	154	24	26	43	86
4	12,533	225	36	38	65	128
5	12,898	321	47	50	87	170
6	13,291	415	60	61	109	211
7	13,688	497	72	73	129	253
8	14,138	581	83	84	150	295
9	14,607	668	94	96	172	339
10	15,122	756	106	107	195	384

†Production below capacity.

155

Table 6.5.2. Times Series of Expansion of Capacity in the 22 Sectors, for the Model with Consumption Proportionality, Restricted Maximal Capacity Growth (10%) and Minimal Growth in Consumption (1%).

Sector	I	II	III	IV	V	VI	VII	VIII
1	170	66	71	–	–	1,251	–	237
2	295	516	701	150	207	1,615	135	381
3	307	646	941	269	365	1,776	257	347
4	470	650	863	295	479	1,954	334	425
5	446	699	957	325	473	2,149	425	431
6	438	736	1,025	358	461	2,364	468	448
7	472	780	1,125	393	502	2,601	515	480
8	511	839	1,236	386	546	2,861	566	517
9	552	899	1,308	420	560	3,147	335	555
10	–	–	–	–	–	–	–	–

Sector	IX	X	XI	XII	XIII	XIV	XV	XVI
1	98	25	–	–	1,084	–	22	168
2	812	217	304	1,236	1,893	260	104	155
3	894	365	334	1,359	2,082	342	119	163
4	983	401	367	1,495	2,291	340	125	170
5	1,081	441	404	1,645	2,520	368	133	179
6	1,190	486	445	1,809	2,772	569	140	184
7	1,309	534	489	1,990	3,049	417	314	193
8	1,440	588	538	2,189	3,354	450	263	201
9	1,584	647	592	2,408	3,689	487	380	212
10	–	–	–	–	–	–	–	–

Sector	XVII	XVIII	XIX	XX	XXI	XXII
1	106	82	12	14	25	45
2	303	71	11	11	17	41
3	393	71	11	12	21	42
4	365	96	11	11	22	41
5	392	93	12	11	21	41
6	397	82	11	11	20	41
7	449	84	11	11	21	42
8	469	86	11	11	21	43
9	514	88	11	11	22	45
10	–	–	–	–	–	–

average annual growth rates of sectoral capacity only two exceptions. The first one is the growth of the production capacity of the Other Market Services sector, which doubled from 1 percent to 2 percent annually, to provide for the increase of this sector's consumption. Since the capital coefficient in this sector is relatively high, satisfying this demand is expensive. The second exception is the growth of the capacity of the Metal Products sector, which remains at its upper bound of 10 percent. This sector is now the only one for which the restriction on maximal growth of capacity is binding all the time. In the preceding section, this was the case for not less than seven sectors. The growth rates of sectoral capacities are shown in the following table.

	Sectoral Growth Rates			
Sector	Average Annual Growth Rate	Sector		Average Annual Growth Rate
I Agriculture	5%	X	Paper	8%
II Energy	5%	XI	Various Products	8%
III Ores	5%	XII	Building	8%
IV Minerals	8%	XIII	Commerce	9%
V Chemical Products	4%	XIV	Transport	4%
VI Metal Products	10%	XV	Money Affairs	4%
VII Means of Transport	6%	XVI	Other Market Services	2% ↑
VIII Foods	3%	XVII	Administration	3%
IX Textiles	8%			

The required increase of consumption places heavy burdens on the system especially in the first year. The system reacts with a sectoral excess capacity in the first year that is much larger than in the three preceding runs. In fact, one might say that nearly the whole burden of the increase of consumption is charged against the first year. Most sectors are included in the list of sectors for which relative excess capacity is more than 1 percent, and what's more, one observes enormous rates of excess capacity in the Minerals, Means of Transport, Various Products and Building sectors, the sectors that act as buffers absorbing the tensions again and again. It is remarkable that in later years the system also finds advantages in providing the Textiles and Paper sectors with excess capacity—the Textiles sector even at a considerable rate.

		Sectoral Excess Capacity				
	Sector	*Year 1*	*Year 2*	*Year 3*	*Year 4*	*Year 5*
II	Energy	7%	—	—	—	—
III	Ores	11%	—	—	—	—
IV	Minerals	32%	11%	7%	—	—
V	Chemical Products	7%	—	—	—	—
VI	Metal Products	15%	—	—	—	—
VII	Means of Transport	19%	4%	—	—	—
IX	Textiles	1%	—	7%	14%	3%
X	Paper	6%	—	—	3%	6%
XI	Various Products	20%	6%	8%	—	—
XII	Building	45%	18%	15%	3%	1%
XIII	Commerce	3%	4%	—	—	—
XIV	Transport	6%	—	—	—	—
XV	Money Affairs	4%	—	—	—	—
XVII	Administration	3%	—	—	—	—
	Total	10%	2%	2%	1%	0%

Among the shadow prices on the political restrictions there is one extreme outlier; the shadow price in the first year for the Other Market Services sector amounts to nearly 600 EUR. This sector is the only one of the conventional sectors that produces at full capacity in the first year to meet the required 1-percent increase in final consumption. However, this sector is not capable of simultaneously supplying other sectors with sufficiently large intermediate deliveries. Production in the other sectors, therefore, has to fall. Because the intermediate deliveries are small in the Other Market Services sector in comparison with final demand, a given increase in final demand has relatively great consequences for the performance of the system. Here, in particular, we find the explanation of the severe general decline of production during the first year and at the same time the explanation of the huge shadow price, because mitigating this restriction provides the system with many opportunities for growth.

Regarding the development of sectoral consumption, the table of its time series seems to be more instructive than that of the shadow prices on the political restrictions once again. The series in question are presented in Table 6.5.3. There is a great resemblance between the corresponding Tables 6.5.3 and 6.4.3; the pattern of consumption above the (rising) minimal level is especially similar. The same sectors deliver the additional consumption goods required to meet the consumption-proportionality restriction. The quantities of these goods have, of

Table 6.5.3. Time Series of Final Consumption in the 22 Sectors for the Model with Consumption Proportionality, Restricted Maximal Capacity Growth (10%) and Minimal Growth in Consumption (1%).

Sectors	I	II	III	IV	V	VI	VII	VIII
1	2,151	2,201	—	161	1,070	1,616	1,111	9,352
2	2,172	2,223	—	163	1,081	1,632	1,122	9,446
3	2,194	2,246	—	164	1,092	1,648	1,133	9,540
4	2,216	2,268	—	166	1,103	1,925†	1,144	9,635
5	2,238	2,291	—	168	1,114	2,449†	1,207†	9,732
6	2,261	2,314	—	173†	1,125	3,036†	1,267†	9,829
7	2,283	2,337	—	209†	1,136	3,776†	1,454†	9,927
8	2,306	2,360	—	250†	1,147	4,567†	1,605†	10,027
9	2,329	2,384	—	252	1,159	5,566†	1,780†	10,127
10	2,352	2,408	—	255	1,170	5,622	1,798	10,228

Sectors	IX	X	XI	XII	XIII	XIV	XV	XVI
1	4,141	616	1,373	242	11,655	1,605	757	9,382
2	4,182	622	1,387	244	11,771	1,621	765	9,476
3	4,224	628	1,401	247	13,909†	1,638	772	9,571
4	4,266	634	1,603†	2,647†	15,425†	1,654	780	9,667
5	5,486†	641	1,683†	3,602†	17,160†	1,671	788	9,763
6	6,336†	946†	1,778†	4,715†	19,083†	1,687	796	9,861
7	7,021†	1,090†	1,903†	5,598†	21,241†	1,885†	804	9,960
8	7,775†	1,247†	2,041†	6,743†	23,616†	1,904	891†	10,059
9	8,605†	1,425†	2,196†	7,843†	26,249†	1,923	948†	10,160
10	8,691	1,439	2,218	14,050†	26,511	1,943	957	10,261

Table 6.5.3. (Continued)

Sectors	XVII	XVIII	XIX	XX	XXI	XXII
1	9,322	521	92	79	80	224
2	9,415	469	83	71	72	202
3	9,509	422	75	64	65	182
4	9,604	380	67	57	58	163
5	9,700	342	60	51	52	147
6	9,797	307	54	46	47	132
7	9,895	277	49	42	42	119
8	9,994	249	44	37	38	107
9	10,094	224	39	34	34	96
10	10,195	201	35	30	31	87

[†]Consumption above minimal level.

160

course, been reduced because the lack of balance of consumption is redressed somewhat by the new political restrictions.

The objections against the development of sectoral consumption, raised in the preceding section, are still partially valid. A minimal increase in sectoral consumption of but 1 percent is insufficient to eliminate these objections completely, and an increase larger than 1 percent leads to an infeasible problem. To escape from this dilemma, restrictions limiting the increase of sectoral consumption could be incorporated into the model as well. It is our opinion, however, that no new insight would be gained by this exercise.

With the model in its present form (run 4), the system produces time series of sectoral production and consumption that might be considered reasonably acceptable on the whole. The wage sum grows at a rate of 6 percent per annum. This growth rate is large enough to afford scope for the introduction of additional desiderata into the model by adding new restrictions. The feasibility and costs of such new demands on the system can be investigated. We shall give a specific example in the next section of this chapter.

6.6   RESTRICTIONS ON THE CONSUMPTION OF ENERGY

In this section we give a specific example illustrating the way the model of run 4 can be used as a relations-bank. We shall introduce relations that represent restrictions on the consumption of energy. Here we have strengthened the restriction limiting the increase of the production capacity of Sector II (Energy). In the previous run of the model this increase was limited to 10 percent annually, at which level the restriction was inactive. In the present run the limit is fixed at 2 percent yearly, in conformity with the Carter Energy Plan. This run, therefore, will reflect some aspects of the Carter proposals. We will show that the introduction of the new restriction is bound to exert a strong influence on the system. To some extent, however, the severity of the impact will be mitigated in actual practise by elimination of some obvious waste of energy, especially in the domain of final consumption.

In the preceding section the average annual growth rate of the capacity of the Energy sector was 5 percent. The growth rate of final consumption of energy was at its required minimal level of 1 percent, thus intermediate deliveries of energy grew on the average at a rate of about 6 percent annually. As the growth of capacity is being forced back from 5 to 2 percent, while the minimal increase of final consumption is left unchanged, the growth rate of the intermediate deliveries has to fall drastically from 6 to a little more than 2 percent.

Referring to the energy row (the second one) of the technology matrix for the Region, it will be obvious at once that all 22 sectors are conspicuous users of energy, in some cases on a relatively large scale. Technical coefficients over .04

Table 6.6.1. Time Series of Actual Production in the 22 Sectors for the Model with Consumption Proportionality, Restricted Maximal Capacity Growth (10%) – Energy Sector only 2% – and Minimal Growth in Consumption (1%).

Sector	I	II	III	IV	V	VI	VII	VIII
1	6,995†	9,507†	11,518†	1,780†	6,538†	12,449†	2,819†	13,296†
2	7,238	10,304†	12,895†	2,542	7,010	14,900	3,261†	13,536
3	7,419	10,580	13,015	2,726	7,176	14,887†	3,078†	13,712
4	7,569	10,792	13,061†	2,801†	7,288	14,782†	3,132†	13,876
5	7,708	11,008	13,193†	2,820	7,389	15,127†	3,222†	14,042
6	7,856	11,228	13,369	2,809†	7,499	15,686	3,353†	14,215
7	8,029	11,453	13,514	2,823	7,632	16,091	3,441†	14,396
8	8,216	11,682	13,666	2,834	7,778	16,525	3,531	14,585
9	8,443	11,915	13,773	2,849	7,958	16,793	3,594	14,788
10	8,673	12,154	13,846	2,931	8,130	16,793	3,594	14,980

Sector	IX	X	XI	XII	XIII	XIV	XV	XVI
1	7,954†	3,207†	2,469†	7,289†	17,281†	6,467†	2,486†	9,650
2	8,138	3,453	3,014†	12,360	18,133	6,884	2,613†	9,817
3	8,665	3,587	3,157	13,596	18,355	7,038	3,121	9,950
4	8,944	3,702	3,239	14,051	18,553	7,150	3,433	10,102
5	9,106	3,825	3,292	14,051	18,798	7,263	3,777	10,233
6	9,353	3,951	3,336	13,812†	19,075	7,377	4,155	10,355
7	9,841	4,078	3,394	13,764†	19,341	7,498	4,570	10,493
8	10,465	4,208	3,451	13,688†	19,619	7,621	5,027	10,632
9	11,511	4,342	3,514	13,650†	19,885	7,751	5,530	10,773
10	12,662	4,475	3,588	14,130	19,967	7,888	6,083	10,912

Sector	XVII	XVIII	XIX	XX	XXI	XXII
1	11,420†	—	—	—	—	—
2	11,918	85	13	15	29	48
3	13,013	155	23	24†	45†	77†
4	14,314	215	32†	32†	56†	102†
5	15,745	270	40†	40†	66†	125†
6	17,141	322	48	47†	75	147†
7	18,402	374	56	53	84	167
8	19,602	425	62	59	93	187
9	20,725	480	69	65	102	205
10	21,819	534	75	71	112	223

†Production below capacity.

are observed in the Ores, Minerals, Chemical Products and Transport sectors as
well as in all abatement sectors. The lowest coefficient (for the Money Affairs
sector) is still over .01. It goes without saying that restricting the growth rate of
intermediate deliveries of energy that much will affect the system profoundly.
In the long run, the limited expansion of the production capacity of the Energy
sector will jeopardize further expansion in all other sectors. It is to be expected
that the system will direct expansion of production capacity mainly towards
those sectors that use relatively little energy, with the Money Affairs sector as an
obvious candidate.

Under the newly added restriction on energy consumption, economic growth
still remains possible, although at a low level. We found an average annual
growth rate of 3 percent for the sum of wages, to be compared with 6 percent in
Section 6.5. It is doubtful whether in actual practise any growth can be achieved,
because the time paths of sectoral investments, the system devised in order to
obtain the maximal value of the objective function, are more involuted than ever
before. Tables 6.6.1 and 6.6.2 show the time paths of actual production and
expansion of the capacity, respectively, for the 22 sectors. The average annual
growth rates of actual production per sector are shown in the following table.

	Sectoral Growth Rates			
Sector	*Average Annual Growth Rate*		*Sector*	*Average Annual Growth Rate*
I Agriculture	2%	X	Paper	3%
II Energy	2%	XI	Various Products	2%
III Ores	1%	XII	Building	2%
IV Minerals	2%	XIII	Commerce	1%
V Chemical Products	1%	XIV	Transport	2%
VI Metal Products	1%	XV	Money Affairs	10% ↑
VII Means of Transport	0%	XVI	Other Market Services	1%
VIII Foods	1%	XVII	Administration	8% ↑
IX Textiles	3%			

The growth rates do not exceed 3 percent except for two cases. The first one
regards the Money Affairs sector, tipped earlier as a fast expanding sector, which
grows at its maximal rate of 10 percent. Moreover, the Administration sector is
expanding fast as well. The growth rates of these two sectors are not only larger
than they were in the preceding section, but they are the largest for all runs of

Table 6.6.2. Time Series of Expansion of Capacity in the 22 Sectors for the Model with Consumption Proportionality, Restricted Maximal Capacity Growth (10%) — Energy Sector only 2% — and Minimal Growth in Consumption (1%).

Sector	I	II	III	IV	V	VI	VII	VIII
1	188	203	—	2	0	—	—	236
2	181	207	55	184	165	—	—	175
3	149	211	170	93	112	290	—	164
4	138	215	183	—	101	—	—	165
5	148	220	—	—	109	496	—	172
6	172	224	145	2	132	404	—	181
7	187	229	152	10	145	433	1	188
8	227	233	106	15	179	267	63	203
9	229	238	72	81	172	—	—	191
10	—	—	—	—	—	—	—	—

Sector	IX	X	XI	XII	XIII	XIV	XV	XVI
1	108	43		—	238	44	258	167
2	527	133	117	1,236	221	153	283	133
3	279	115	82	455	198	112	312	152
4	161	122	52	—	244	112	343	130
5	247	126	44	—	277	114	377	122
6	488	126	57	—	265	120	415	138
7	623	129	57	—	277	123	457	139
8	1,046	134	63	—	265	129	502	140
9	1,151	132	73	79	82	137	553	139
10	—	—	—	—	—	—	—	—

Sector	XVII	XVIII	XIX	XX	XXI	XXII
1	188	85	13	15	29	48
2	1,094	69	10	38	41	100
3	1,301	60	25	—	3	—
4	1,431	54	—	—	—	—
5	1,395	52	—	—	—	—
6	1,260	52	7	—	9	18
7	1,200	51	6	6	8	19
8	1,122	55	6	5	9	18
9	1,094	53	6	5	9	17
10	—	—	—	—	—	—

the model discussed in this chapter. In all other sectors there is a considerable decline in the growth rate, most pronounced in the Means of Transport sector, where no growth at all is observed in the period of interest.

There are other remarkable developments to be obtained from Table 6.6.1. The pattern of excess capacity has changed during the last years of the period of interest in comparison with the situation described in the preceding section. Structure and size of excess capacity in the first year remain unaffected, but from the second year on excess capacity is now only present in the Means of Transport sector (during the entire period of interest) and in four of the five abatement sectors. Pollution abatement absorbs enormous amounts of energy. During the second and third years the system built larger installations than required, obviously because this is favourable in terms of the objective function. But having built them, the system declines to use them at full capacity—which would entail exceeding the minimal requirements regarding pollution control— because this would be too expensive in terms of energy. The complete list of sectoral excess capacity over 1 percent, is contained in the following table.

	Sector	Year 1	Year 2	Year 3	Year 4	Year 5	Year 6	Year 7
	Sectoral Excess Capacity							
II	Energy	7%	—	—	—	—	—	—
III	Ores	11%	—	—	—	1%	—	—
IV	Minerals	30%	—	—	—	—	—	—
V	Chemical Products	7%	—	—	—	—	—	—
VI	Metal Products	16%	—	—	3%	—	—	—
VII	Means of Transport	20%	8%	13%	11%	9%	5%	3%
X	Paper	6%	—	—	—	—	—	—
XI	Various Products	19%	—	—	—	—	—	—
XII	Building	41%	—	—	—	—	2%	2%
XIII	Commerce	3%	—	—	—	—	—	—
XIV	Transport	5%	—	—	—	—	—	—
XV	Money Affairs	4%	8%	—	—	—	—	—
XVII	Administration	3%	—	—	—	—	—	—
XIX	Private Waste Water Treatment	—	—	—	33%	17%	—	—
XX	Desulphurization	—	—	55%	40%	25%	11%	—
XXI	Solid Waste Management	—	—	36%	23%	10%	—	—
XXII	Adaptation of Cars	—	—	48%	31%	16%	—	—
	Total	9%	0%	0%	1%	0%	0%	0%

All the particularities of the time series of sectoral actual production are more or less reflected in the time series of sectoral expansion of capacity (see Table 6.6.2). Except for the Energy sector itself and for the Money Affairs sector, very irregular patterns are found. It is remarkable that the time series give the impression of being generated at random, while in fact they are the result of a very careful optimization procedure.

It is evident that in the present run of the model, the 2-percent restriction on the expansion of the capacity of the Energy sector is binding all the time, with shadow prices gradually declining from 45 EUR in the first year to 4 EUR in the seventh year. The restriction on the capacity expansion in the Money Affairs sector (10%) is binding all the time as well, but the shadow prices on this restriction are much lower; they do not exceed 2 EUR.

Final Consumption and Restrictions on the Consumption of Energy

The fact that the development of sectoral final consumption is completely different from that described in the preceding section is a consequence of the unequal shifts in the growth rates of sectoral production. According to the proportionality restriction (introduced in run 2), total consumption has to grow at least at the same rate as the sum of wages. In the case of Section 6.5, this meant at a rate of 6 percent and in the present case at a rate of 3 percent. Furthermore, according to the restrictions on balanced growth of consumption (introduced in run 4), the annual increase of final consumption has to be at least 1 percent in every sector. In the preceding section we observed that not all sectors contribute proportionally to the surplus in consumption that results from the proportionality restriction. Additional consumption goods were delivered mainly by the Metal Products, Textiles, Building and Commerce sectors. In the present run the consumers are once more provided with (a small amount of) Textiles and with the services of the Money Affairs and Administration sectors.

The table on page 169 contains the composition of the additional consumption basket in the seventh year, that is, at the end of the period of interest. The situation in which the consumption of energy is restricted (run 5) is contrasted with the situation without this limitation (run 4). The figures read in billions of EUR. The conclusion to be drawn from all this must be that if society wants to maintain some economic growth in the face of a restriction on the consumption of energy, a shift of the consumption pattern in the direction indicated by the results of the computer run seems unavoidable. Although there remains a certain lack of balance in the growth of consumption, we have the feeling that the pattern of additional consumption in the present run of the model is the most realistic one in the five runs we have shown. It may even have some prognostic

Table 6.6.3. Time Series of Final Consumption in the 22 Sectors for the Model with Consumption Proportionality, Restricted Maximal Capacity Growth (10%) — Energy Sector only 2%—and Minimal Growth in Consumption (1%).

Sectors	I	II	III	IV	V	VI	VII	VIII
1	2,151	2,201	—	161	1,070	1,616	1,111	9,352
2	2,172	2,223	—	163	1,081	1,632	1,122	9,446
3	2,194	2,246	—	164	1,092	1,648	1,133	9,540
4	2,216	2,268	—	166	1,103	1,664	1,144	9,635
5	2,238	2,291	—	168	1,114	1,681	1,156	9,732
6	2,261	2,314	—	169	1,125	1,698	1,167	9,829
7	2,283	2,337	—	171	1,136	1,715	1,179	9,927
8	2,306	2,360	—	173	1,147	1,732	1,191	10,027
9	2,329	2,384	—	174	1,159	1,749	1,203	10,127
10	2,352	2,408	—	176	1,170	1,767	1,215	10,228

Sectors	IX	X	XI	XII	XIII	XIV	XV	XVI
1	4,141	616	1,373	242	11,655	1,605	757	9,382
2	4,182	622	1,387	244	11,771	1,621	765	9,476
3	4,502[†]	628	1,401	247	11,889	1,638	988[†]	9,571
4	4,665[†]	634	1,415	249	12,008	1,654	1,122[†]	9,667
5	4,751[†]	641	1,429	252	12,128	1,671	1,271[†]	9,763
6	4,892[†]	647	1,443	254	12,249	1,687	1,436[†]	9,861
7	5,188[†]	654	1,458	257	12,372	1,704	1,618[†]	9,960
8	5,570[†]	660	1,472	259	12,496	1,721	1,820[†]	10,059
9	6,224[†]	667	1,487	262	12,621	1,738	2,043[†]	10,160
10	6,287	673	1,502	890[†]	12,747	1,756	2,064	10,261

Sectors	XVII	XVIII	XIX	XX	XXI	XXII
1	9,322	521	92	79	81	225
2	9,415	469	83	71	73	203
3	10,306[†]	422	75	64	65	182
4	11,469[†]	380	67	57	59	164
5	12,764[†]	342	60	51	53	148
6	14,024[†]	308	54	46	48	133
7	15,138[†]	277	49	42	43	119
8	16,186[†]	249	44	37	38	107
9	17,149[†]	224	39	34	35	97
10	18,060[†]	202	35	30	31	87

[†] Consumption above minimal level.

Composition of Additional Consumption Basket (Year 7).

Sector	Run 4	Run 5
VI Metal Products	2.1	—
VII Means of Transport	0.3	—
IX Textiles	2.6	0.8
X Paper	0.4	—
XI Various Products	0.4	—
XII Building	5.3	—
XIII Commerce	8.9	—
XIV Transport	0.2	—
XV Money Affairs	—	0.8
XVII Administration	—	5.2
Total additional consumption	20.2	6.8

value for a society, aiming at a high level of employment, that also plans to limit its consumption of energy, in the sense that there is an indication of where the main stresses are going to be produced.

6.7 EPILOGUE

In recent years the principle of optimization in economic models has come under severe attack. Simon[3] introduced the concept of "bounded rationality" and confronted the optimization principle with the concept of "satisficing behaviour".[4] It is not appropriate at this time to take sides in this discussion about the fundamentals of microeconomics.[5]

We must concede that the Neoclassicists saw the optimization principle as an abstraction, never to be observed in reality without some dilution by other aspirations. They, too, realised that the actual process of decision making is but very imperfectly approximated by a maximization process. Formally, the main attraction of the maximization principle is of course the great wealth of theorems that can be derived starting from this assumption. We believe, however, that one serious flaw inherent to that principle has been overlooked in the discussion about the pros and cons of it.

The preceding analysis has amply demonstrated the all-pervading monomania that characterizes behaviour based on the maximization principle. The amazing ingenuity and the unacceptable rigour, the insensitivity for all aspects of reality not included in the objective function, which are the consequence of the adoption of maximizing behaviour, are undoubtedly some of the reasons that the reality contents of the neoclassical theory do not seem to be overly great.

We began by naively introducing a rather simple model and were immediately confronted with the fact that the solution presented by the system showed traits that were unacceptable. We then introduced restrictions that prevented the system from going too far in that direction and found that the system had gone off in another direction that was equally undesirable and equally unexpected. Afterwards, that is, after we had seen the solution, the system's behaviour was perfectly obvious. But to predict in advance the devious paths the system found to maximize its objective function is another matter.

Traditionally, the theory of the firm is of a static character and therefore these traits of the optimizing behaviour have not received much attention. But as soon as one analyses dynamic behaviour, these aspects are the first ones that catch the eye. We have adapted the system by sequentially introducing new restrictions until we possessed a model that showed satisfactory behaviour. This process implies a distribution of the importance attached to the different aspects of the behaviour of the system that might be too one-sided. The newly introduced restrictions have to be satisfied first and only then will the space left be used to optimize the objective function.

It would, of course, have been possible to introduce a multiobjective criterion by weighing these aspects in some manner and including them in the objective function. But we have the feeling that it is impossible to visualize all the important aspects in advance. A much better approach seems to us to be the interactive one as advocated for instance by Nijkamp and Spronk.[6] They state: "An interactive variant of goal programming can circumvent the obvious difficulty of obtaining complete a priori information about the decision makers preference function". This is a point of view with which we wholeheartedly agree.

NOTES

CHAPTER 1

1. This nomenclature is called NACE-CLIO (Nomenclature général des Activités dans les Communautés Européennes; Classification Input-Output).

2. See R. Dorfman, P.A. Samuelson and R.M. Solow. *Linear Programming and Economic Analysis.*

3. See E. Malinvaud. "Aggregation Problems in Input-Output Models".

4. See SOEC. *Regional Statistics, 1972.*

5. See K.O. Kymn. "Interindustry Energy Demand and Aggregation of Input-Output Tables".

6. See, e.g., H.H. Harman. *Modern Factor Analysis.*

7. See P. Whittle. "On Principal Components and Least Square Methods".

8. See J.H.P. Paelinck et al. *Etude comparée des tableaux d'entrées et de sorties des Communautés Européennes.*

9. See e.g. P.W.M. John. *Statistical Design and Analysis of Experiments.*

10. This assumption is not entirely valid. Columnwise the technical coefficients and the primary inputs add up to 1. If one has n mutually independent drawings of the stochastic variable x and defines the technical coefficients e_1 and e_2 as follows:

$$e_1 = \frac{x_1}{x_1 + \cdots + x_n} \quad \text{and} \quad e_2 = \frac{x_2}{x_1 + \cdots + x_n}$$

then e_1 and e_2 are dependent. We can prove that the correlation coefficient $R(e_1, e_2)$ is about $-1/(n - 1)$ if the x's are mutually independent. We have decided to ignore this correlation of the order of magnitude n^{-1}.

11. It must be assumed that ϵ_{Ijk} and $\epsilon_{I'j'k}$ $(I \neq I'$ and $j \neq j')$ are mutually independent, an assumption not entirely valid for $I \neq I'$ but $j = j'$. See also note 10.

12. This problem is closely related to the one called "Multiple Comparisons". See R.G. Miller, Jr. *Simultaneous Statistical Inference.*

13. See P.A. Samuelson. *Economics* (9th ed.).

CHAPTER 2

1. See S. Chakravarty. *Capital and Development Planning.*

2. See J. Clark and S. Cole, *Global Simulation Models.*

3. "Selective Growth", a paper prepared by the Dutch Ministry of Economic Affairs, is an excellent example.

4. Op. cit. Section 6.8.

5. See O. Rademaker. "World Models and Forecasting; a Control Engineering Perspective".

6. See e.g. V. Ginsburgh and J. Waelbroeck. "A General Equilibrium Model of World Trade, pt. III", or Y. Kaya et al. "Future of Global Interdependence". In the first paper the two kinds of relations are combined into one model. In the FUGI project the Japanese authors have linked a static input-output model to a dynamic macroeconomic one.

7. See R.M. Goodwin. "A Growth Cycle".

8. J. Clark and S. Cole op. cit.

9. See O. Lange. *Optimal Decisions; Principles of Programming.*

10. See P. Nijkamp and J. Spronk. "Interactive Multiple Goal Programming; Method and Application".

11. Op. cit.

12. See H. Kahn. *Thinking about the Unthinkable.*

13. See M. Mesarovic and E. Pestel. *Mankind at the Turning Point.*

14. Quoted from G. Hupkes (our translation).

15. See Tj.C. Koopmans. *Linear Regression Analysis of Economic Time Series.*

16. See I.M.T. Stewart. "Economic Prediction and Human Action".

17. See R.M. Goodwin. "Static and Dynamic Linear Equilibrium Models".

18. IPES. "Modellbanksystem (MBS) Leistungsbeschreibung".

19. See W. Müller and C.B. Tilanus. "Linear programming from a management point of view; A survey, Netherlands 1976".

CHAPTER 3

1. For a list of these sectors see Appendix 4A.

2. See Tj.C. Koopmans. "Analysis of Production as an Efficient Combination of Activities".

3. See V. Ginsburgh and J. Waelbroeck. "A General Equilibrium Model of World Trade, Part III".

4. Mr. J.W. Eelkman Rooda did some computations with the model in an adapted form. His findings are that a period of optimization of 10 years is not a bad choice if the period of interest is 5 to 7 years.

5. Op. cit. Section 2.3.

CHAPTER 4

1. In the principal component solution this statement is the analogue of the decomposition theorem of a symmetric positive definite matrix.

2. In that year consisting of Germany, France, Italy, The Netherlands, Belgium and Luxemburg. For this last country no tables were available.

3. The index of factorization is defined as:

$$100 \sum_{j=1}^{m} \sum_{i=1}^{M} l_{ij}^2 / m$$

4. There are 56 branches, thus 56 columns, but one of them (number 56) consisted of only 0s and was therefore omitted from the analysis.

5. A factor loading of .6 contributes on the average to about one-half of the variance explained by the 15 factors together.

6. See the footnote in Appendix 4D.

7. Compound Vortex Controlled Combustion.

8. See Central Planning Bureau of The Netherlands. *Monograph no. 20.*

9. See S. Kuznets. *Economic Growth of Nations; total output and production structure.*

CHAPTER 5

1. The adjustments of the model, necessary to obtain feasible solutions, namely the introduction of enforced investments in the abatement sector, eliminated the necessity of a positive value of this capacity. Nevertheless, we left the initial conditions unaltered.

2. In accordance with the change in the rate of decrease for allowed nuisance from 10 percent to 5 percent, the initial value for f_4 was changed from 833.33 to 789.47 letting the value 750 for f_4 in the first year unchanged.

CHAPTER 6

1. The total wage sum consists of gross salaries and wages, inclusive of employers' social welfare contributions.

2. We prefer to study production capacity rather than actual production. The growth rates of the latter variables are inflated in most sectors, production being below capacity in the first (few) years.

3. See H. Simon. "A Behavioural Model of Rational Choice".

4. See R.M. Cyert and J.G. March. *A Behavioural Theory of the Firm.*

5. *Modern Microeconomics*, by A. Koutsoyiannis, contains a survey of the arguments.

6. See P. Nijkamp and J. Spronk. "Goal Programming for Decision-making".

BIBLIOGRAPHY

Central Planning Bureau of The Netherlands. *Monograph no 20:* Economische Gevolgen van Bestrijding van Milieu Verontreiniging ("Economic Consequences of Pollution Abatement"). The Hague: Staatsuitgeverij, 1975.

Chakravarty, S. *Capital and Development Planning.* Cambridge, Mass: The MIT Press, 1969.

Clark, J., and Cole, S. *Global Simulations Models, a comparative study* (with Curnow, R. and Hopkins, M.). London: Wiley, 1975.

Cyert, R.M., and March, J.G. *A Behavioural Theory of the Firm.* London: Prentice-Hall, 1973.

Dorfman, R., Samuelson, P.A., and Solow, R.M. *Linear Programming and Economic Analysis.* New York: McGraw-Hill, 1958.

Ginsburgh, V., and Waelbroeck, J. "A General Equilibrium Model of World Trade, Part III". *Center for Operations Research & Econometrics.* Heverlee-Belgium: Catholic University of Louvain, 1977.

Goodwin, R.M. "Static and Dynamic Linear General Equilibrium Models", in *Input-output Relations* (ed. The Netherlands Economic Institute). Leiden: H.E. Stenfert Kroese N.V., 1953.

Goodwin, R.M. "A Growth Cycle" in C.H. Feinstein (ed.) *Capitalism, Socialism and Economic Growth.* Cambridge: University Press 1967. Reprinted in E.K. Hunt and J. Schwartz (eds.) *A Critique of Economic Theory.* Penguin, 1972.

174

Harman, H.H. *Modern Factor Analysis*. Chicago and London: The University of Chicago Press, 1967.

Institut für Planungs- und Entscheidungssysteme (IPES). "Modellbanksystem (MBS) Leistungsbeschreibung". Internal Report (77.203). Bonn, 1977.

John, P.W.M. *Statistical Design and Analysis of Experiments*. New York: The Macmillan Company, 1971.

Kahn, H. *Thinking about the Unthinkable*. New York: Horizon press, 1962.

Kaya, Y. et al. "Future of Global Interdependence". *Proceedings of the 5th Global Modelling Conference*. Laxenburg-Austria: International Institute for Applied Systems Analysis (IIASA), 1977.

Koopmans, Tj.C. *Linear Regression Analysis of Economic Time Series*. Haarlem – The Netherlands: De Erven F. Bohn N.V., 1937.

Koopmans, Tj.C. "Analysis of Production as an Efficient Combination of Activities". In Tj.C. Koopmans (ed.) *Activity Analysis of Production and Allocation*. New York: John Wiley and Sons, 1951.

Koutsoyiannis, A. *Modern Microeconomics*. London: The Macmillan Press Ltd, 1975.

Kuznets, S. *Economic Growth of Nations; total output and production structure*. Cambridge, Mass.: Harvard University Press, 1971.

Kymn, K.O. "Interindustry Energy Demand and Aggregation of Input-Output Tables". *The Review of Economics and Statistics*, vol. LIX, August 1977.

Lange, O. *Optimal Decisions; Principles of Programming*. Oxford e.a.: Pergamon Press, 1971.

Malinvaud, E. "Aggregation Problems in Input-Output Models", in T. Barna (ed.) *The Structural Interdependence of the Economy*. New York: John Wiley and Sons, 1954.

Mesarovic, M., and Pestel, E. *Mankind at the Turning Point*, The second Report to The Club of Rome. New York: E.P. Dutton & Co., Inc./Reader's Digest Press, 1974.

Miller, R.G., Jr. *Simultaneous Statistical Inference*. New York: McGraw-Hill, 1966.

Ministerie van Economische Zaken ("Dutch Ministry of Economic Affairs") *Selectieve Groei, economische structuurnota ("Selective Growth")*. The Hague: Staatsuitgeverij, 1976.

Müller, W., and Tilanus, C.B. "Linear Programming from a Management Point of View; A survey, Netherlands 1976". *European Journal of Operations Research*, no. 2, 1978.

Nijkamp, P., and Spronk, J. "Goal Programming for Decision-making", *Centrum voor Bedrijfseconomisch Onderzoek*. Rotterdam: Erasmus University, 1977 (preliminary discussion paper).

Nijkamp, P., and Spronk, J. "Interactive Multiple Goal Programming; Method and Application". *Proceedings of the International Conference on Operations Research*, Toronto, 1978.

Paelinck, J.H.P. et al. *Etude comparée des tableaux d'entrées et de sorties des*

Communautés Européennes. Namur: Facultés Universitaires Notre-Dame de la Paix, 1966.

Rademaker, O. "World Models and Forecasting; a Control Engineering Perspective", *Journal A,* vol. 16; no. 4, 1975.

Samuelson, P. A. *Economics.* 9th ed. New York e.a.: McGraw-Hill, 1973.

Simon, H. "A Behavioural Model of Rational Choice". *Quarterly Journal of Economics,* 1955.

Statistical Office of the European Communities. *Regional Statistics,* Luxemburg: office for official publications of the European Communities, 1972.

Stewart, I.M.T. "Economic Prediction and Human Action". *Futures,* vol. 7, April 1975.

Whittle, P. "On Principal Components and Least Square Methods". *Skandinavisk Aktuari Tidskrift,* 1952.

INDEX